Artificial Intelligence in the Developer's World: A New Paradigm

Summary Table of Contents

Contents

Detailed Table of Contents

Preface

- Introduction to the concept of AI in software development.

- Overview of the book's purpose and target audience.

Chapter 1: Introduction to Artificial Intelligence

- Definition and evolution of AI.

- Core concepts and technologies in AI (Machine Learning, Neural Networks, etc.).

- The role of AI in the modern world.

Chapter 2: AI and Software Development: An Overview

- The intersection of AI and software development.

- Key benefits and challenges of integrating AI in software development.

- Case studies of successful AI integration in software development.

Chapter 3: AI in Software Design and Prototyping

- AI-driven approaches to software design.

- Automated prototyping tools.

- Enhancing user experience (UX) design with AI.

Chapter 4: AI in Coding and Programming

- Automated code generation.

- AI-assisted programming tools.

- Machine learning in algorithm optimization.

Chapter 5: AI in Testing and Quality Assurance

- Automated testing tools powered by AI.

- AI in bug tracking and fixing.

- Enhancing software reliability with AI.

Chapter 6: AI in Project Management

- AI for project planning and risk assessment.

- AI tools for team collaboration and communication.

- Predictive analytics in project management.

Chapter 7: AI in Deployment and Maintenance

- AI in continuous integration and deployment (CI/CD).

- AI for real-time monitoring and maintenance.

- Predictive maintenance using AI.

Chapter 8: AI in Security

- AI in cybersecurity and threat detection.

- Automated vulnerability assessment.

- AI in compliance and data privacy.

Chapter 9: Ethical Considerations and Challenges

- Ethical implications of AI in software development.

- Addressing bias and fairness in AI applications.

- The future of employment in the age of AI-driven software development.

Chapter 10: The Future of AI in Software Development

- Emerging trends and technologies.

- Potential future applications and innovations.

- Preparing for an AI-augmented software development landscape.

Conclusion

- Recap of key insights and takeaways.

- The ongoing evolution of AI in software development.

Appendices

- Glossary of AI and software development terms.

- Resources for further reading and learning.

- Interviews with industry experts.

References

- A list of all sources used in the research and composition of the book.

Index

Preface

Introduction to the Concept of AI in Software Development

In the ever-evolving landscape of technology, artificial intelligence (AI) has emerged as a revolutionary force, redefining the boundaries of what is possible. At the intersection of this transformative journey is software development, a field that has been fundamentally reshaped by the advent of AI. This book delves into the profound impact AI has on software development, exploring how algorithms and machine learning models are not just tools in the hands of developers but collaborators that redefine the creation, testing, and deployment of software.

AI in software development signifies a paradigm shift from traditional coding practices to a more intelligent, data-driven approach. This transformation encompasses everything from automated code generation and enhanced debugging processes to predictive analytics in project management and sophisticated AI-driven security protocols. The integration of AI is not merely a matter of adding a layer of intelligence to existing processes but represents a rethinking of how software is conceptualized, created, and maintained.

Overview of the Book's Purpose and Target Audience

The purpose of this book is twofold. Firstly, it serves as a comprehensive guide for those looking to understand the role of AI in modern software development practices. It offers insight into the current state of AI in this field, its applications, benefits, challenges, and ethical considerations. Secondly, the book aims to provide a vision of the future, exploring emerging trends and potential advancements that AI might bring to software development.

This book is intended for a diverse audience, ranging from software developers, engineers, and IT professionals seeking to integrate AI into their workflows, to students and educators in computer science and related fields. It is also an invaluable resource for business leaders and technology strategists who need to understand how AI can give their organizations a competitive edge in software development. Furthermore, this book is suitable for anyone with a keen interest in the intersection of AI and software development, regardless of their technical background.

In the following chapters, we will embark on a journey through the various dimensions of AI in software development. From the fundamentals of AI technologies to their practical applications and ethical implications, this book aims to provide a thorough understanding of how AI is reshaping the landscape of software development and what the future might hold in this exciting field.

About the Author

Bernard Baah, the CEO of a globally expanding software development company, Filly Coder, is the accomplished author of "Artificial Intelligence in the Developers World." With a vast background in Cyber Security, Machine Learning, AI, Networking, Digital Marketing, and other advanced technologies, Baah brings a rich array of practical and strategic insights. His vision to transform Filly Coder into a global technology leader is deeply intertwined with his commitment to harnessing innovative technologies to enhance business efficiency and customer engagement across various industries.

Baah offers a unique global perspective on the integration of AI into software development. This perspective is enriched by his company's diverse portfolio, which includes specialized management systems for sectors such as education and hospitality, and innovative platforms like Filly Tutor and Filly Jobs.

Bernard is also deeply invested in fostering the next generation of tech talent through initiatives like NextGen FillyCamp and Filly Bootcamp, where emerging developers are trained in state-of-the-art technologies. His hands-on experience in developing custom software solutions and platforms provides invaluable real-world context to the discussions in this book.

"Artificial Intelligence in the Developers World" draws upon Bernard Baah's extensive technical knowledge and leadership experiences, as well as his firsthand insights into the operational challenges and breakthroughs that accompany the integration of AI into various software development processes. The book aims to equip software developers, IT professionals, and business leaders with the knowledge and tools necessary to navigate and excel in the AI-augmented landscape of modern software development.

Visit Filly Coder (https://fillycoder.com) for more information on Bernard's initiatives and follow him on social media to stay updated on the latest in technology and business:

Website: https://fillycoder.com

Twitter: twitter.com/fillycoder

Twitter: twitter.com/bbaah123

YouTube: youtube.com/@fillycoder9793

Instagram: instagram.com/fillycoder

TikTok: tiktok.com/@bernardbaah

LinkedIn: linkedin.com/company/18100059

Facebook: facebook.com/fillycoder

Chapter 1: Introduction to Artificial Intelligence

Definition of AI

Artificial Intelligence, commonly abbreviated as AI, is a branch of computer science dedicated to creating systems capable of performing tasks that typically require human intelligence. These tasks include learning from experiences, recognizing patterns, solving complex problems, understanding natural language, and adapting to new or evolving environments. AI encompasses a range of technologies, from simple automated response systems to complex machine learning and neural networks, capable of self-learning and decision-making.

The core of AI lies in its ability to mimic cognitive functions associated with the human mind, such as learning and problem-solving. This capability is not limited to replicating human thought processes, but also extends to performing tasks more efficiently and accurately than humans.

Evolution of AI

The evolution of AI can be traced back to the mid-20th century, when the idea of creating intelligent machines first emerged. The term "Artificial Intelligence" was coined in 1956 by John McCarthy, a computer scientist, during the Dartmouth Conference. The initial phase of AI research in the 1950s and 1960s was marked by optimism and significant advancements, such as the development of the first AI programs capable of playing checkers and solving algebra problems.

However, the field faced its first major setbacks in the 1970s, a period known as the "AI Winter," due to inflated expectations, lack of funding, and technical limitations. Despite these challenges, the 1980s and 1990s saw a resurgence of interest in AI, spurred by the advent of more powerful computers and the development of machine learning algorithms.

The real breakthrough came in the 21st century with the rise of big data and advanced computational power. The introduction of deep learning and neural networks has led to remarkable achievements in AI, such as mastering complex games such as Go, driving autonomous vehicles, and enabling highly accurate voice and image recognition.

This evolution has not been linear, but rather a series of advancements, setbacks, and rejuvenations. Today, AI stands at the forefront of technological progress, with its potential applications spanning across various sectors, from healthcare and finance to education and entertainment.

As we delve deeper into this book, we will explore how AI, emerging from its complex history, is now an integral part of modern software development, reshaping the landscape with its unique capabilities.

Core Concepts and Technologies in Artificial Intelligence

1. Machine Learning (ML)

- **Definition:** Machine Learning is a subset of AI that involves the development of algorithms that can learn and make predictions or decisions based on data. This learning process is automated and improves with experience, without being explicitly programmed for each task.

- **Key Techniques:**

- Supervised Learning: Algorithms learn from labeled training data, allowing them to predict outcomes for unforeseen data.

- Unsupervised Learning: Algorithms identify patterns and relationships in data without any labels.

- Reinforcement Learning: Algorithms learn to make decisions by performing actions and assessing the outcomes.

2. Neural Networks and Deep Learning

- **Neural Networks:** Inspired by the human brain, neural networks consist of layers of interconnected nodes or neurons that process data and can learn complex patterns. They are fundamental in many AI applications.

- **Deep Learning:** An advanced form of machine learning, deep learning utilizes deep neural networks. This involves many layers of neurons, allowing for the processing of vast amounts of data and the recognition of intricate patterns, making it highly effective for tasks like image and speech recognition.

3. Natural Language Processing (NLP)

- **Definition:** NLP is a field at the intersection of computer science, artificial intelligence, and linguistics. It involves the development of algorithms that understand, interpret, and generate human language.

- **Applications:** This includes speech recognition, language translation, sentiment analysis, and chatbots.

4. Computer Vision

- **Definition:** Computer vision is an AI field that trains computers to interpret and process the visual world. By using digital images and deep learning, machines can accurately identify and classify objects — and react to what they "see."

- **Applications:** Facial recognition, object detection in autonomous vehicles, and medical image analysis.

5. Robotics and AI

- **Definition:** Robotics combines AI with physical machines, allowing for the creation of robots that can perform tasks autonomously.

- **Applications:** Industrial automation, drones, and robotic process automation in various sectors.

6. Predictive Analytics

- **Definition:** This involves using historical data, machine learning, and statistical algorithms to predict future outcomes.

- **Applications:** Risk assessment, market trends analysis, and customer behavior forecasting.

7. AI Ethics and Bias

- **Considerations:** As AI technologies advance, ethical considerations, such as data privacy, algorithmic bias, and the impact of AI on employment, are increasingly important.

- **Bias Mitigation:** Efforts to create fair and unbiased AI systems are central to responsible AI development.

Each of these core concepts and technologies plays a critical role in the field of AI, offering unique capabilities that drive innovation and efficiency. In the context of software development, understanding these technologies is key to leveraging AI's full potential.

The Role of AI in the Modern World

Artificial Intelligence (AI) has emerged as a transformative force in the modern world, reshaping industries, influencing daily life, and altering the way we interact with technology. Its impact is extensive, touching on numerous sectors and aspects of life.

In the realm of business and industry, AI has revolutionized processes by optimizing business operations, automating routine tasks, and improving operational efficiencies. This leads to significant cost savings and increased productivity. Additionally, AI's prowess in processing and analyzing large volumes of data aids in more informed decision-making, identifying trends, and predicting consumer behavior.

Healthcare has also seen substantial advancements thanks to AI. Tools powered by AI assist in diagnosing diseases more accurately and swiftly, often recognizing patterns that might be missed by human experts. These technologies also play a critical role in personalizing treatment plans for patients and have accelerated the drug development process, from discovery to clinical trials, reducing time and costs.

In the field of education, AI enables personalized learning experiences by adapting materials and pacing to suit individual student needs, thereby enhancing the educational process. It also automates administrative tasks for educational institutions, freeing educators to focus more on teaching and less on paperwork.

Transportation is another sector where AI has made significant inroads. Autonomous vehicles, driven by AI, aim to reduce human error and increase road safety. Additionally, AI algorithms are employed to optimize traffic flow and public transportation systems, reducing congestion and improving efficiency.

The retail and e-commerce sector has been transformed by AI through personalization and recommendation systems that tailor the shopping experience based on consumer behavior and preferences. AI also optimizes inventory levels and supply chain operations, leading to cost savings and improved customer satisfaction.

In environmental conservation, AI models are crucial for predicting climate change trends and assessing the impact of various environmental policies. They also aid in monitoring wildlife and detecting illegal activities such as poaching and deforestation.

The entertainment and media industry is witnessing AI's influence in content creation, including the generation of music, art, and written content. AI also curates personalized content in streaming services, enhancing user experience.

Moreover, AI's social impact is notable. Initiatives focused on 'AI for Good' tackle societal challenges ranging from disaster response to food security. However, the widespread adoption of AI also raises important questions about ethics, privacy, job displacement, and the digital divide, necessitating ongoing dialogue and regulation.

In conclusion, AI's role in the modern world is expansive and continually evolving. It offers substantial benefits and efficiencies across various sectors, while concurrently presenting new challenges and ethical considerations. Understanding these diverse impacts is crucial for harnessing AI's potential in a responsible and effective manner.

The Intersection of AI and Software Development

As we embark on exploring the intersection of AI and software development, it's crucial to understand how these two fields, once distinct, are now increasingly intertwined, leading to revolutionary changes in the way software is designed, developed, and deployed.

1. Enhanced Software Development Lifecycle

- **AI in Planning and Requirements Analysis:** AI tools can analyze requirements and provide recommendations, enhancing the planning phase with data-driven insights.

- **Design and Prototyping:** AI-driven design tools allow for more efficient prototyping, offering automated suggestions for layout and user experience.

- **Coding and Programming:** AI assists in code generation, error detection, and even in writing unit tests, speeding up the development process and reducing manual effort.

- **Testing and Quality Assurance:** Automated testing powered by AI not only speeds up the process but also leads to more thorough and accurate results, improving software quality.

- **Deployment and Maintenance:** AI in continuous integration and continuous deployment (CI/CD) pipelines enables smarter deployment strategies and predictive maintenance, foreseeing potential issues before they impact users.

2. AI-Driven Development Tools

- **Intelligent Coding Assistants:** Tools like AI-powered Integrated Development Environments (IDEs) assist developers by suggesting code improvements, identifying bugs, and providing documentation support.

- **Automated Code Reviews:** AI systems can review code for quality, security, and compliance, offering immediate feedback and learning from past reviews to improve future analysis.

3. AI in Software Design

- **User Experience Optimization:** AI algorithms analyze user behavior to guide the development of more intuitive and user-friendly interfaces.

- **Adaptive Interfaces:** AI enables the creation of dynamic user interfaces that adapt to individual users' preferences and needs.

4. AI in Project Management

- **Resource Allocation and Risk Assessment:** AI helps in predicting project timelines, assessing risks, and optimally allocating resources.

- **Team Collaboration and Management:** AI-driven tools enhance team collaboration, providing insights into team dynamics and workflow efficiencies.

5. The Role of Data in AI-Driven Software Development

- **Data-Driven Decision Making:** AI leverages data from various sources, including user feedback and application performance, to guide development decisions.

- **Predictive Analytics:** Predictive models forecast trends and user needs, allowing for proactive software enhancements.

6. The Synergy of AI and DevOps

- **AI in Continuous Improvement:** Integrating AI with DevOps practices enables continuous learning and improvement, aligning software development more closely with business objectives.

- **Automated Operations:** AI automates and optimizes operations, reducing manual intervention and increasing efficiency.

The intersection of AI and software development represents a paradigm shift towards more intelligent, efficient, and user-centric software creation. This synergy not only enhances the technical aspects of development but also aligns software products more closely with user needs and business goals.

Key Benefits and Challenges of Integrating AI in Software Development

Benefits of AI Integration

1. **Increased Efficiency and Productivity:** AI automates routine tasks, speeds up the development cycle, and reduces manual errors, leading to increased productivity and efficiency in software development processes.

2. **Enhanced Quality and Accuracy:** AI algorithms can analyze and test software at a deeper level than humanly possible, leading to improved software quality and reliability.

3. **Data-Driven Insights:** AI's ability to process and analyze vast amounts of data helps in making informed decisions, predicting user behavior, and tailoring software to meet user needs more effectively.

4. **Innovative Solutions and Creativity:** AI opens up new possibilities for innovative software solutions, pushing the boundaries of traditional software development with advanced capabilities like natural language processing and predictive analytics.

5. **Scalability and Flexibility:** AI-driven processes can easily scale according to project needs, offering flexibility in managing resources and adapting to changing requirements.

Challenges of AI Integration

1. **Complexity and Technical Expertise:** Implementing AI in software development requires specialized knowledge and skills, which can be a barrier for teams without AI expertise.

2. **Data Quality and Availability:** AI systems require large amounts of high-quality data to train and function effectively. Obtaining, managing, and processing this data can be challenging.

3. **Ethical and Privacy Concerns:** Integrating AI raises concerns about user privacy, data security, and ethical use of AI, which need to be carefully managed.

4. **Integration with Existing Systems:** Integrating AI into existing software development processes and legacy systems can be complex and resource-intensive.

5. **Risk of Bias and Inaccuracy:** AI systems can inadvertently learn biases present in their training data, leading to biased or inaccurate outcomes.

6. **Cost Implications:** The initial investment for integrating AI, including infrastructure and training costs, can be significant, which might be a hurdle for smaller organizations.

7. **Ongoing Maintenance and Updates:** AI models require continuous monitoring, updating, and retraining to stay effective, which demands ongoing resources and expertise.

8. **Change Management:** Adopting AI in software development often requires significant changes in workflows and processes, which can be met with resistance and requires effective change management strategies.

While the integration of AI in software development offers numerous benefits like efficiency, quality improvement, and innovation, it also presents challenges related to complexity, data management, ethical considerations, and costs. Navigating these benefits and challenges effectively is crucial for organizations looking to harness the power of AI in their software development endeavors.

Case Studies of Successful AI Integration in Software Development

Case Study 1: Automated Bug Detection and Resolution

- **Company:** A leading tech corporation.

- **Challenge:** The company faced challenges in identifying and resolving bugs efficiently in its large codebase.

- **Solution:** They implemented an AI system that could scan the entire codebase, identify potential bugs, and suggest fixes. The system used machine learning algorithms trained on historical bug data and resolutions.

- **Outcome:** The AI system significantly reduced the time taken to identify and fix bugs, improving software quality and reducing the workload on the development team.

Case Study 2: AI-Driven Personalized User Experience

- **Company:** A global e-commerce platform.

- **Challenge:** The company wanted to enhance user engagement by providing personalized experiences to its users.

- **Solution:** They integrated AI to analyze user behavior, preferences, and purchase history to provide personalized product recommendations and content.

- **Outcome:** This AI-driven personalization led to an increase in user engagement and sales, as users found the platform more relevant to their individual needs.

Case Study 3: Predictive Analytics for Project Management

- **Company:** A software development agency.

- **Challenge:** The agency struggled with project delays and budget overruns due to inefficient project management.

- **Solution:** The agency adopted AI-powered predictive analytics tools to forecast project timelines, identify potential risks, and optimize resource allocation.

- **Outcome:** The implementation of AI in project management resulted in more accurate project timelines, better risk management, and cost savings.

Case Study 4: AI in Continuous Integration and Deployment (CI/CD)

- **Company:** A cloud services provider.

- **Challenge:** The company aimed to enhance its CI/CD pipeline for faster and more efficient software releases.

- **Solution:** They employed AI to automate various stages of the CI/CD pipeline, including code integration, testing, and deployment decisions.

- **Outcome:** This led to a significant reduction in manual errors, faster deployment times, and an overall increase in the efficiency of the software release process.

Case Study 5: Enhancing Code Quality with AI

- **Company:** A financial software firm.

- **Challenge:** The firm needed to ensure high code quality and compliance with financial regulations.

- **Solution:** They integrated an AI-based code review tool that could analyze code for quality, security, and compliance with regulatory standards.

- **Outcome:** The AI tool improved code quality, ensured compliance, and saved time for the development team by automating the code review process.

AI-Driven Approaches to Software Design

The integration of AI into software design is significantly transforming how designers approach the conceptualization and prototyping of software applications. These AI-driven methods are not just enhancing efficiency; they are also fostering new avenues for creativity and innovation in the field of software design.

AI-powered tools are increasingly being utilized in UI/UX design, enabling the automatic generation of design elements based on best practices and user data. These tools provide suggestions for layout, color schemes, and user flow, greatly aiding the design process. Additionally, AI accelerates the prototyping phase, allowing designers to rapidly generate functional prototypes from initial design inputs. This rapid prototyping facilitates quicker testing and iteration of designs.

A user-centered design approach is another area where AI is making a significant impact. AI algorithms analyze user data to understand preferences and behaviors, leading to the creation of personalized user experiences. This ensures that designs are focused on the user, catering to the specific needs of different user segments. AI is also employed to enhance the accessibility of software designs, making applications more usable for people with various disabilities and suggesting design modifications to improve readability, navigation, and interaction.

Predictive design is another revolutionary aspect of AI in software design. AI's capability to anticipate future trends and user needs allows designers to create designs that are adaptable to changing user expectations. AI also enables the development of adaptive user interfaces that adjust in real-time based on user interactions, context, and preferences, thus offering a dynamic and responsive user experience.

Collaboration in design teams is being reshaped by AI-driven design tools. These platforms enhance team collaboration, even when members are distributed across different locations. They provide suggestions for design improvements, maintain version control, and streamline the feedback process. Moreover, AI tools analyze feedback from user testing sessions, offering valuable insights that can be directly incorporated into the design process.

In the realm of design optimization and testing, AI is playing a crucial role. It automates the process of A/B testing and quickly analyzes results, leading to data-driven design decisions that improve the user experience. AI tools also assess the performance of different design elements, optimizing them for various devices and platforms to ensure consistency and reliability across user interfaces.

In conclusion, AI-driven approaches are reshaping the landscape of software development. By automating routine tasks, enabling personalization of user experiences, and enhancing team collaboration, AI is empowering designers to focus more on innovation and creativity. This shift is leading to the development of more effective and user-friendly software products, marking a new era in software design.

AI tools relating to AI in Software Design and Prototyping:

1. **Adobe Sensei:** Adobe Sensei An AI and machine learning platform that powers intelligent features across all Adobe products, enhancing creativity and design workflows.

1. **Autodesk's Dreamcatcher:** Project Dreamcatcher An AI-assisted design system that allows designers to input design goals and other parameters to generate design alternatives.

2. **Sketch2Code by Microsoft:** Sketch2Code - Microsoft AI Lab This tool uses AI to convert hand-drawn sketches into HTML code, facilitating rapid prototyping of web designs.

3. **Figma's Design Systems Analytics:** An AI-powered tool that helps design teams analyze how design systems are used and make informed decisions about design changes.

4. **Wix's ADI (Artificial Design Intelligence):** A platform that creates unique, personalized websites based on user input, streamlining web design processes.

5. **Airtable Blocks:** Introducing Airtable Blocks This tool offers AI-driven features like image tagging and text enrichment to enhance data organization and management in design projects.

6. **Canva's Magic Resize:** Canva Magic Switch An AI feature within Canva that automatically adapts designs to different formats and sizes, saving time in creating multiple versions of a design.

7. **Zeplin:** An AI-enabled collaboration tool for designers and developers, facilitating the transition from design to development with automated style guides and resources.

8. **Uizard:** An AI-powered design tool that specializes in transforming wireframes into user interface designs, streamlining the transition from ideation to digital design.

9. **Zecoda:** This tool converts Photoshop designs into front-end code using AI, significantly speeding up the development process.

10. **DeepArt:** An AI tool that applies artistic styles to designs, allowing for creative experimentation with visuals.

11. **Runway ML:** A platform for creatives to use machine learning tools in their design process, enabling novel design approaches and visual effects.

12. **Fontjoy:** An AI tool that helps designers in selecting and pairing fonts using deep learning to ensure aesthetic compatibility.

13. **Let's Enhance:** A tool that uses AI to enhance image resolution without losing quality, useful in refining design visuals.

14. **Designs.ai Logomaker:** An AI-driven tool that assists in creating unique logos by learning from user preferences and design trends.

These AI tools represent a range of applications, from automating design tasks to enhancing creative processes, and they are instrumental in modernizing and streamlining software design and prototyping.

AI Tool in Focus: Sketch2Code

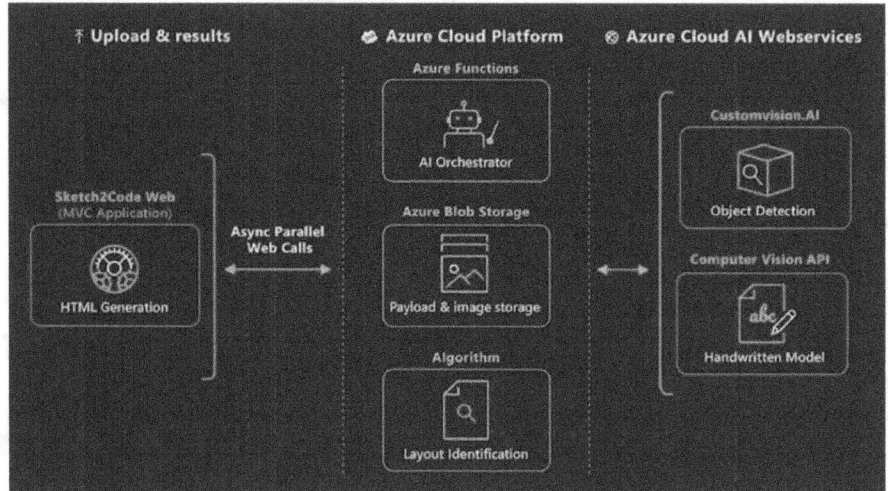

Sketch2Code is an innovative tool developed by Microsoft, leveraging artificial intelligence to convert hand-drawn sketches into working HTML prototypes. This technology is particularly beneficial for developers, as it allows them to transform hand-drawn or wireframe sketches into functional HTML code, streamlining the process of turning visual ideas into digital realities.

The way Sketch2Code operates is quite straightforward and user-friendly. Users begin by uploading an image of their hand-drawn sketch to the Sketch2Code website. This can be done either by uploading a pre-existing image file or by taking a photo of the sketch. Once the image is uploaded, the tool's AI technology, specifically a custom vision model, analyzes the sketch. This AI model is prebuilt to recognize various UI elements and patterns in the sketches. After analyzing the image, Sketch2Code converts the visual elements into corresponding HTML code.

The technology behind Sketch2Code is a remarkable example of how AI can be utilized to bridge the gap between traditional design processes and modern web development. It simplifies the transition from conceptual sketches to working digital formats, thereby accelerating the design and development workflow. This tool is especially useful for rapidly creating prototypes and bringing ideas to life in a digital format without the need for manually writing all the underlying code

Here's a general overview of how Sketch2Code works:

1. **Input**: Users create hand-drawn sketches or wireframes of a web page design on paper or digitally using a stylus or touchpad.

2. **Image Capture**: The sketches are then captured using a camera or uploaded as image files.

3. **AI Processing**: Microsoft's AI algorithms analyze the images and recognize the visual elements, such as buttons, text fields, images, and layouts, based on patterns and shapes.

4. **Code Generation**: After analyzing the sketches, the AI generates corresponding HTML code, CSS styles, and layout structures that match the design. The AI tries to interpret the intent of the designer and translate it into functional code.

5. **Output**: The resulting HTML and CSS code can be downloaded and used as a starting point for web development. Developers can further customize and refine the generated code to suit their needs.

Sketch2Code is an example of how AI can be applied to streamline specific aspects of software development, in this case, web design and front-end development. It can save time for designers and developers by automating the initial code creation process based on visual designs. However, it's important to note that while AI can assist in code generation, manual coding and refinement are often necessary to create a polished and responsive web application.

Automated Prototyping Tools in Software Design

The integration of automated prototyping tools, powered by AI, has significantly streamlined the process of software design, enabling rapid development, testing, and refinement of prototypes. These tools utilize AI algorithms to automate and enhance various aspects of the prototyping process.

Here's a comprehensive overview of various AI tools that can be used in different aspects of the design and development process:

1. **Rapid Prototype Generation**

   - **Taskade: An AI-powered tool designed to enhance workflow and expedite the prototyping process. It provides efficiency by offering ready-to-use templates and intuitive features.**

   - **Uizard: Offers rapid, AI-powered UI design for creating wireframes, mockups, and prototypes. It can generate UI designs from text prompts, convert hand-drawn sketches into wireframes, and transform screenshots into editable designs.**

   - **Visily: Known for its speed in prototyping, it turns paper sketches into wireframes and prototypes. Visily stands out for converting sketches into high-quality outputs and has time-saving features like auto-populating labels, names, numbers, and images.**

   - **RAPYD.AI: Allows building AI prototypes or MVPs using AI services from Google, Amazon, and Microsoft. It is designed for quick start-ups and integrates easily with these major AI services.**

2. **Interactive Prototyping**

   - **Figma: Offers a free prototyping tool to build interactive prototypes and mockups. It integrates with tools like Maze and Flinto for additional prototyping and user testing capabilities.**

   - **ProtoPie: Enables the creation of interactive, realistic prototypes for various platforms. Known for its advanced prototyping tool for dynamic and multimodal interactions.**

   - **Proto.io: Helps build interactive web and mobile prototypes with low or high fidelity. It offers drag-and-drop templates and UI components for rapid prototyping.**

- **Framer:** An AI-powered design tool for creating interactive prototypes. It features drag-and-drop interactive components, adaptive layouts, and built-in tools for paging, scrolling, and navigation.

3. **Design Consistency Checks**

   - **Design Copilot AI:** A cutting-edge UI/UX evaluation platform that leverages AI to ensure consistency in design elements across different screens and functionalities.

4. **Feedback Integration**

   - **VisualEyes:** An AI-powered design feedback tool that uses eye-tracking technology and machine-learning algorithms to analyze user interactions with designs. It provides heatmaps and gaze plots for user interaction analysis.

5. **Adaptive Design Iterations**

   - **Midjourney:** Its AI evolves with each design iteration, refining its feedback mechanism for continuous improvement in designs.

6. **Integration with Development Tools**

   - **Grit.io:** Simplifies and automates software maintenance tasks, addressing issues like technical debt. It integrates with platforms like GitHub and VS Code.

   - **Google Cloud AI Platform:** A suite of tools for the entire machine learning lifecycle, facilitating the integration of AI in software development.

   - **AskCodi:** An AI-powered code assistant, aiding in code generation, unit test creation, documentation, and code conversions. Integrates with IDEs like Visual Studio Code and JetBrains.

   - **Tabnine:** Enhances productivity in software development with AI-powered code suggestions. Integrates with most modern IDEs.

   - **Adrenaline AI:** Streamlines the debugging process for developers and integrates with various programming languages and frameworks.

7. **Efficiency in Resource Use**

   - AI tools in general automate routine tasks in prototyping, saving time and resources, and allowing teams to focus on more complex and creative aspects of design.

For more information on these tools, you can visit their respective websites:

- Taskade
- Uizard
- Visily
- RAPYD.AI

- Figma

- ProtoPie

- Proto.io

- Framer

- Design Copilot AI

- VisualEyes

- Midjourney

- Grit.io

- Google Cloud AI Platform

- AskCodi

- Tabnine

- Adrenaline AI

Automated prototyping tools represent a significant advancement in the field of software design, offering efficiency, enhanced user experience, and improved design quality. As AI technology continues to evolve, these tools are expected to become even more sophisticated, further revolutionizing the software design process.

Enhancing User Experience (UX) Design with AI

The integration of Artificial Intelligence (AI) in UX design is revolutionizing the way designers create interfaces, making them more intuitive, user-friendly, and engaging. AI's role in enhancing UX is multifaceted and profoundly influential.

One of the key contributions of AI in UX is the personalization of user experiences. AI algorithms analyze user data and behavior to customize interfaces, content, and functionality according to individual user preferences. This leads to a significant increase in user engagement and satisfaction. Additionally, AI's ability to predict user behaviors and preferences enables designers to anticipate user needs effectively, creating designs that are more likely to meet user expectations.

AI-driven tools are also transforming user testing and usability studies. These tools can conduct automated user testing, quickly gathering and analyzing user feedback, which helps in identifying areas for improvement in the design. Moreover, AI facilitates the creation of adaptive user interfaces that dynamically adjust in real-time based on user interaction, context, and environmental factors, resulting in a more responsive and intuitive user experience.

AI plays a crucial role in enhancing accessibility in designs, making them more inclusive for all users, including those with disabilities. It suggests design adjustments that improve readability and navigability. Furthermore, AI accelerates the iterative process of UX design, allowing for rapid prototyping and testing, which reduces the time and cost involved in developing optimal design solutions.

Innovative interaction modes such as voice, gesture, and even emotion recognition are being explored thanks to AI, broadening the scope of user engagement with software. AI is also instrumental in content optimization. It analyzes how users engage with content and assists in optimizing the placement, format, and type of content that resonates best with users.

In summary, AI is a game-changer in UX design, significantly enhancing the process by enabling personalization, predictive analysis, and the development of innovative interaction models. These advancements are leading to more user-centric and engaging software applications, marking a new era in the field of UX design.

Here's a list of AI tools for enhancing user experience (UX) design, along with their respective URLs:

1. **Framer**: A tool well-known for its user-friendly no-code platform and advanced prototyping features. Framer

2. **Uizard**: Helps automate design tasks, focusing on high-level strategy and creativity. Uizard

3. **ChatGPT**: Used for generative content creation and converting data into actionable insights. ChatGPT

4. **Jasper**: Aids in brand-focused content creation and optimization. Jasper

5. **Fronty**: The world's first image to HTML converter, useful for no-code and low-code design. Fronty

6. **Khroma**: An AI-powered color palette generator for sleek and trendy design aesthetics. Khroma

7. **Visualeyes**: Offers AI-powered tools for user testing, including eye-tracking studies and preference tests. Visualeyes

8. **Visily**: Allows creation of wireframes and prototypes from hand-drawn sketches and other inputs. Visily

9. **Adobe Sensei**: Brings AI capabilities to design, automating tasks and offering creative suggestions. Adobe Sensei

10. **Attention Insight**: Provides user-testing tools for validating design concepts using predictive analytics. Attention Insight

AI Tool in Focus: Framer

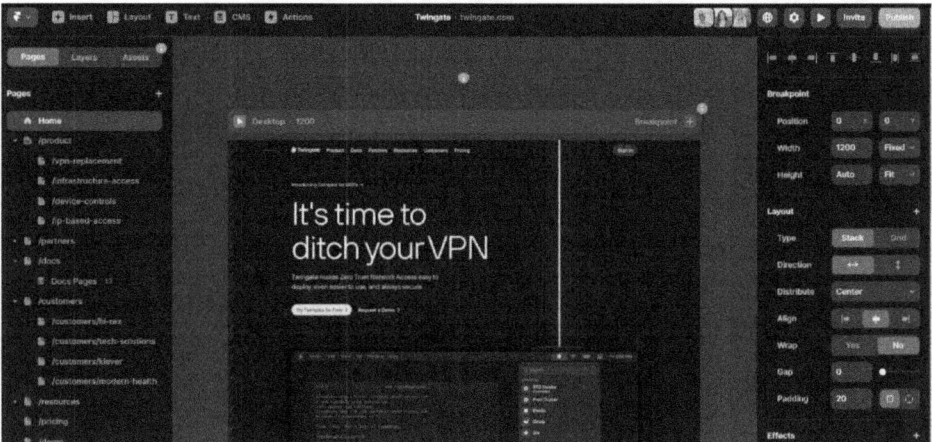

Framer is a versatile tool primarily used for interactive design, particularly in UI and UX design. It offers a range of features and capabilities:

1. **Interactive Design Platform**: Framer is known for its powerful capabilities in building interactive UI/UX designs. It allows designers to create complex animations and interactions for web and mobile applications. This includes the ability to prototype designs that can simulate real-world user interactions, providing a more realistic and dynamic preview of how the design would function in practice.

2. **Collaborative Environment**: The platform offers features that support teamwork and collaboration. Multiple team members can work on the same project simultaneously, making it easier to integrate work from designers, copywriters, and developers. This collaborative approach is beneficial in coordinating efforts and ensuring consistency across different stages of the design process.

3. **Ease of Use**: Framer is known for its user-friendly interface, which is accessible to designers of all skill levels. While it offers advanced features for experienced designers, it also provides an approachable learning curve for beginners. This makes it a popular choice for both professional design teams and individuals who are just starting out in the field of digital design.

4. **Integration with Other Tools**: Framer integrates well with other design and development tools. This interoperability is essential for a smooth workflow, allowing designers to import designs from other platforms and export their Framer projects to formats suitable for development or further refinement.

5. **Community and Resources**: Framer has a strong community of users and offers a wealth of resources, including templates, tutorials, and forums. This community support is invaluable for learning new techniques, troubleshooting issues, and staying updated on the latest trends in UI/UX design.

6. **Customization and Flexibility**: The tool allows a high degree of customization, enabling designers to tailor their projects to specific needs. This includes the ability to create custom

components and utilize a wide range of design assets, enhancing the creative possibilities available to users.

Framer is a comprehensive tool that caters to the modern needs of UI/UX design, offering a blend of powerful features, ease of use, and collaborative capabilities. Its focus on interactivity and user experience makes it a go-to choice for designers looking to create sophisticated and user-friendly digital products.

Chapter 4: AI in Coding and Programming

Automated Code Generation

The advent of AI in coding and programming has led to the development of automated code generation, a process that significantly alters the traditional approach to writing code.

1. **Automated Code Generation**

   - **OpenAI Codex**: It's proficient in over a dozen languages including Python, JavaScript, Go, Perl, PHP, and Ruby, leveraging natural language and billions of lines of source code.

   - **Replit AI**: Assists in generating a full Express server among other tasks, making boilerplate and repetitive code easier to handle.

   - **Tabnine**: An AI-based code completion tool using deep learning algorithms, supporting several programming languages like Java and Python.

   - **Blackbox AI**: Helps in writing code faster, with real-time knowledge of the world, making it able to answer questions about recent events, technologies, etc.

     - OpenAI Codex

     - Replit AI

     - Tabnine

     - Blackbox AI

2. **Advancements in Machine Learning Models**

   - The application of pre-trained language models to code generation, specifically in Python, demonstrates significant improvements in BLEU scores and a better understanding of Python syntax.

     - Automatic Code Generation using Pre-Trained Language Models

3. **Enhancing Developer Productivity**

   - Generative AI tools can significantly increase the speed of common developer tasks such as documenting code functionality, writing new code, and refactoring existing code.

     - Unleash developer productivity with generative AI | McKinsey

4. **Use Cases in Various Programming Languages**

   - **GitHub Copilot**: Powered by OpenAI's GPT-3, assists developers in writing code by providing code completions and explanations in plain English, translating natural language descriptions into code for various programming languages.

   - AI-powered tools for bug detection, test case generation, natural language interfaces for development, code translation, and code refactoring demonstrate versatility across different programming languages.

-

5. **Integration with Existing Development Tools**

- **Grit.io**: Simplifies and automates software maintenance tasks and integrates with platforms like GitHub and VS Code.

- **Google Cloud AI Platform**: Provides a suite of tools for the machine learning lifecycle, supporting diverse frameworks and integrating with the development process.

- **AskCodi**: An AI-powered code assistant, available as an extension for IDEs like Visual Studio Code, Sublime Text, and JetBrains' IDEs.

- **Tabnine**: Enhances productivity with AI-powered code suggestions, integrating with most modern IDEs.

- **Adrenaline AI**: Streamlines the debugging process and supports various programming languages and frameworks, integrating with development tools.

  - Grit.io

  - Google Cloud AI Platform

  - AskCodi

  - Tabnine

  - Adrenaline AI

Each of these tools offers unique functionalities, catering to different aspects of software development and machine learning, enhancing productivity and efficiency in the development process.

Challenges and Considerations

While automated code generation promises efficiency, there are challenges such as ensuring the quality and security of the generated code, and the need for developers to thoroughly understand and maintain AI-generated code.

Automated code generation represents a significant leap forward in the field of coding and programming, offering unprecedented efficiency and the potential to accelerate software development processes. As this technology continues to evolve, it is poised to become an integral part of the software development toolkit.

AI Tool in Focus: Tabnine

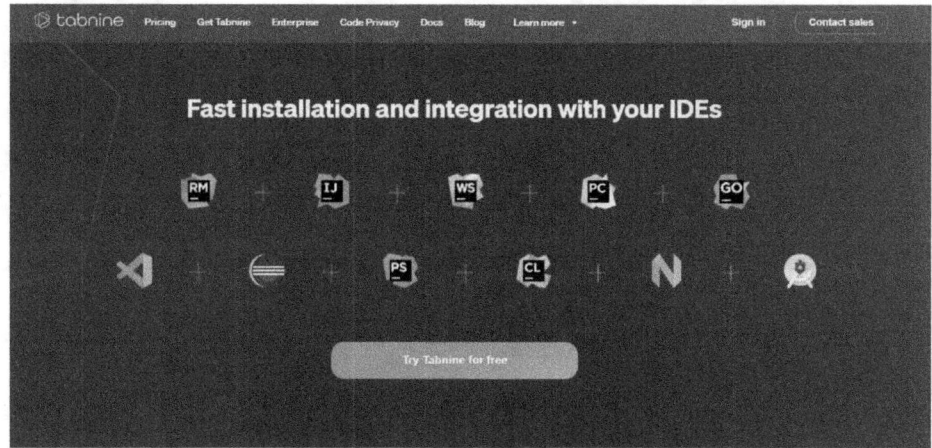

Tabnine is a sophisticated AI code assistant tool that offers various features and functionalities to enhance the software development process:

1. **AI Code Assistant for All Programming Languages**: Tabnine supports all major programming languages and Integrated Development Environments (IDEs). This broad compatibility makes it a versatile tool for developers working with languages like TypeScript, PHP, Java, C++, Go, Rust, and others. Its ability to integrate with various IDEs, such as VS Code and WebStorm, ensures that it caters to a wide range of developer preferences and workflows.

2. **Generative AI for Software Development**: Since its launch in 2018, Tabnine has been at the forefront of applying generative AI in software development. It focuses on boosting code quality and developer satisfaction by automating significant portions of the coding workflow. Tabnine is known to automate 30-50% of code creation for each developer, enhancing productivity and efficiency in the software development process.

3. **AI Pair Programming Tool**: Tabnine functions like a collaborative partner in coding, offering real-time suggestions as developers write code. It is designed to act as a helpful companion inside the IDE, providing guidance and mentorship. This approach to AI-assisted development helps streamline the coding process, although it's important to note that the suggestions by Tabnine may not always be correct. Users are encouraged to understand how to make the tool more helpful and contextually aware.

4. **Machine Learning Models and Code Privacy**: Tabnine operates using multiple language-specialized machine-learning models, which have been trained from the ground up on code. These models are trained on open-source code with permissive licenses, ensuring a broad and ethical learning base. Tabnine offers flexibility in deployment, as its AI completions can run on a developer's laptop, on a server, or in the cloud, with a strong emphasis on maintaining code privacy.

5. **Customizable to Organizational Best Practices**: Unlike some other AI code assistants, Tabnine uses a proprietary Language Learning Model (LLM) which, while less powerful than some top-line models like GPT-4, has the advantage of being customizable to an organization's specific

code repositories. This feature makes Tabnine highly adaptable and capable of providing code suggestions that align with an organization's best practices and conventions.

Tabnine stands out as a powerful AI tool for software development, offering wide language support, generative AI capabilities, real-time coding assistance, a strong focus on code privacy, and customization to fit organizational standards. It is a valuable asset for developers seeking to enhance productivity and code quality in their software development projects.

AI-Assisted Programming Tools

AI-assisted programming tools are revolutionizing the software development process by leveraging artificial intelligence to support and enhance various aspects of programming. These tools bring a multitude of functionalities that aid developers in several key areas of software creation.

One of the primary benefits of these tools is intelligent code suggestions and autocompletion. They dramatically reduce the time and effort required for coding by learning from existing codebases to provide context-relevant recommendations. This feature streamlines the coding process, making it more efficient.

Error detection and correction is another critical area where AI-assisted tools excel. They use AI algorithms to detect errors and anomalies in code more effectively than traditional methods. By suggesting corrections, these tools improve the quality and reliability of the code. Refactoring assistance is yet another advantage offered by AI in programming. These tools suggest improvements in code structure and design, enhancing the efficiency and maintainability of the code.

Automated documentation generation and code annotation are key features that significantly help developers. They make understanding and maintaining codebases much easier, streamlining the development process. Moreover, AI tools are capable of learning and adapting to individual developers' coding styles. This personalization leads to an improved and more intuitive developer experience.

Optimizing software performance is a crucial aspect, and AI-assisted tools excel in this area as well. They analyze code to identify performance bottlenecks and suggest optimizations, thereby enhancing the efficiency of the software. Security checks are an essential part of software development, and AI tools contribute significantly by identifying potential security vulnerabilities in the code. This helps in developing more secure applications.

In summary, AI-assisted programming tools are a significant advancement in the field of software development. They offer a range of capabilities that not only enhance the quality of code but also speed up the development process and improve the overall productivity of developers. These tools are transforming how programmers write, debug, and optimize software, marking a new era in software development.

Here are examples of AI tools for various software development tasks:

Code Suggestions and Autocompletion:

- **IntelliCode**: Part of the Visual Studio Code Marketplace, IntelliCode provides AI-powered code completions.

- **Codeium**: Offers AI-powered code completion and search for various IDEs.

- **GitHub Copilot**: Developed by GitHub and OpenAI, it suggests code snippets using GPT technology.

- **CodeGPT**: Allows selection from various models including OpenAI, Anthropic, and Google Makersuite for code autocompletion.

  - IntelliCode

  - Codeium

  - GitHub Copilot

  - CodeGPT

2. **Error Detection and Correction**:

- **Snyk Code Checker**: A free code security tool powered by AI for detecting and correcting code errors.

- **Free AI Detector by Scribbr**: Detects errors using AI tools like Bard, GPT4, and ChatGPT.

- **ZZZCode AI Bug Detector**: Detects bugs in code online for any programming language.

- **Error-Detection Tool by IEEE Spectrum**: Makes AI mistakes easy to spot.

  - Snyk Code Checker

  - Free AI Detector by Scribbr

  - ZZZCode AI Bug Detector

  - Error-Detection Tool by IEEE Spectrum

3. **Refactoring Assistance**:

- **Refact**: An open-source AI coding assistant for code improvement.

- **Refactory**: Designed to improve code quality and efficiency.

- **OpenRefactor**: A Visual Studio Code extension for AI-assisted code refactoring.

- **Sourcery**: Streamlines repetitive tasks like refactoring code.

  - Refact

  - Refactory

  - OpenRefactor

- Sourcery

4. **Code Documentation and Annotation**:

    - **Docify AI**: Offers code comment and documentation tools.

    - **DocuWriter.ai**: Specializes in automated code and API documentation.

    - **Code Documentation - CodePal**: Provides code documentation assistance.

    - **ScreamingBox**: Lists essential AI tools for code documentation.

        - Docify AI

        - DocuWriter.ai

        - Code Documentation - CodePal

        - ScreamingBox

5. **Learning and Adapting to Coding Styles**:

    - AI code tools like GitHub Copilot and Tabnine learn and adapt to a developer's coding habits, offering personalized coding assistance.

        - GitHub Copilot

        - Tabnine

        - CareerFoundry

6. **Optimizing Performance**:

    - AI tools for code optimization typically analyze code for performance bottlenecks and suggest optimizations. However, specific tools for this category were not identified in the current search.

7. **Security Checks**:

    - AI programming tools like Snyk Code Checker also offer functionalities for identifying potential security vulnerabilities.

        - Snyk Code Checker

Each of these tools provides unique functionalities to improve different aspects of the software development process, from writing and debugging code to enhancing security and performance.

Machine Learning in Algorithm Optimization

Machine learning (ML) has become a pivotal force in the field of software development, particularly in the optimization of algorithms, where it significantly enhances both efficiency and effectiveness. ML techniques are being increasingly employed to analyze and improve the performance of various algorithms. This often involves fine-tuning algorithmic parameters to achieve better efficiency and accuracy.

A notable advancement brought about by ML is the development of adaptive algorithms. These algorithms have the ability to learn and evolve based on the input data they receive, thereby improving their performance over time. This adaptability is crucial in handling the dynamic and complex nature of modern data sets and computational problems.

Another key application of ML in this domain is in predictive analytics. ML-driven predictive models are adept at forecasting outcomes, allowing algorithms to make informed, data-driven decisions. This predictive capability is particularly valuable in scenarios where foresight can significantly enhance the decision-making process.

Resource allocation is another area where ML algorithms are making a substantial impact. They optimize the use of computational resources, which is a critical consideration in large-scale applications. By ensuring the most efficient use of resources, ML algorithms enhance the overall functionality and sustainability of software systems.

Moreover, ML has the capacity to automate problem-solving, especially in complex systems where traditional algorithms may be inadequate. This automation involves identifying problems and developing effective solutions, a process that is particularly valuable in dealing with intricate and multifaceted challenges.

In summary, machine learning is introducing a dynamic aspect to algorithm optimization in software development. It enables algorithms to continuously adapt, learn, and improve, thereby playing a crucial role in the advancement of contemporary software development techniques. This evolving landscape underscores the importance of ML in driving innovation and efficiency in algorithm design and implementation.

Here is a list of AI-assisted programming tools along with their URLs:

1. **GitHub Copilot**: Provides intelligent code suggestions, efficient debugging assistance, and security issue spotting. GitHub Copilot.

2. **Divi AI**: Known for unlimited code generation, HTML/JS generation, and integration with Divi Cloud. Divi AI.

3. **Tabnine**: Offers multilingual code completions, user style adaptation, and code refactoring assistance. Tabnine.

4. **Amazon CodeWhisperer**: An innovative code generator with real-time code recommendations in various IDEs. Amazon CodeWhisperer.

5. **Replit**: Known for its browser-based IDE and the AI-powered code assistant Ghostwriter, providing contextually relevant code suggestions. Replit.

6. **Sourcegraph Cody**: An AI-powered assistant for coding that integrates with popular IDEs and provides context-aware answers for coding queries. Sourcegraph Cody.

7. **AskCodi**: Powered by OpenAI Codex, it offers code generation, programming question answers, and code suggestions. AskCodi.

Chapter 5: AI in Testing and Quality Assurance

Automated Testing Tools Powered by AI

The integration of Artificial Intelligence (AI) into the realm of testing and quality assurance has brought about a revolutionary change in this critical phase of software development. AI-powered automated testing tools have introduced a new level of efficiency, accuracy, and depth to the testing processes.

One of the key features of these tools is the intelligent generation of test cases. AI algorithms are capable of automatically creating test cases that are tailored to the application's requirements and user behavior patterns, ensuring that the testing is comprehensive and covers all necessary aspects. Additionally, these tools excel in automated bug detection. They outperform traditional testing methods by analyzing code, runtime environments, and user interactions to detect bugs and anomalies more effectively.

Predictive analytics is another area where AI-driven testing tools are making a significant impact. They use predictive models to identify high-risk areas in the software, allowing testers to prioritize and focus their efforts on the most critical aspects. This approach ensures that the most important parts of the software are thoroughly tested and secure.

AI also plays a crucial role in automating UI testing. AI-driven tools recognize visual elements and interactions to ensure that the user interface works as intended across various devices and screen sizes. This is particularly important in today's diverse device landscape.

Performance optimization is another benefit of AI in software testing. AI algorithms analyze performance data to identify bottlenecks and suggest optimizations. This not only enhances the software's efficiency but also improves the overall user experience.

Moreover, a significant advantage of AI-powered testing tools is their ability to continuously learn and adapt. They evolve their testing strategies over time, learning from new data, test results, and user feedback. This continuous learning ensures that the testing processes remain effective and up-to-date with the latest trends and requirements.

In summary, AI-powered automated testing tools are significantly enhancing the testing phase of software development. They offer more effective, efficient, and comprehensive testing solutions, thereby improving the overall quality and reliability of software products. This advancement in testing technology is a testament to the transformative power of AI in software development.

AI-powered automated testing tools, each offering unique capabilities to enhance software testing and quality assurance:

1. **Selenium**: A robust and versatile tool, now equipped with AI for more flexibility in test execution. Selenium.

2. **Code Intelligence**: Combines dynamic testing with self-learning AI to identify code flaws and vulnerabilities. Code Intelligence.

3. **Functionize**: Executes end-to-end tests that are self-healing and scalable in the cloud. Functionize.

4. **Testsigma**: Uses AI to make test automation faster, supporting a range of testing needs including web, mobile, and APIs. Testsigma.

5. **Katalon Studio**: Prioritizes UI quality using AI to eliminate false positives and offers visual testing capabilities. Katalon Studio.

6. **Applitools**: A next-gen test automation platform powered by Visual AI, streamlining the creation and maintenance of tests. Applitools.

7. **Eggplant Digital Automation Intelligence**: Employs a model-based digital twin testing strategy with AI for comprehensive coverage. Eggplant.

8. **Digital.ai Continuous Testing**: Offers AI-powered comprehensive coverage for various testing use cases, with cloud-based infrastructure. Digital.ai.

9. **TestCraft**: A Selenium-based solution offering codeless testing with AI/ML technology. TestCraft.

10. **Testim**: Increases test coverage and reduces maintenance through its AI-powered platform. Testim.

11. **mabl**: A low-code AI test automation solution providing reliable end-to-end test coverage. mabl.

12. **Watir**: An open-source web application testing tool based on Ruby, simulating real user interactions. Watir.

13. **Sauce Labs**: Offers low-code automated web testing services, empowering citizen testers with AI-powered systems. Sauce Labs.

14. **Tricentis**: Provides an extensive suite of test automation capabilities, leveraging AI and cloud technologies. Tricentis.

15. **SmartBear VisualTest**: Brings AI-powered visual test automation, integrating with existing UI tests. SmartBear.

16. **ACCELQ**: A cloud-based, AI-powered codeless test automation platform for a range of channels. ACCELQ.

17. **Parasoft**: Offers automated end-to-end testing for quality software delivery at scale. Parasoft.

18. **TestRigor**: Takes a user-centric approach to testing, focusing on what needs to be tested without the burden of coding. TestRigor.

These tools provide a comprehensive range of functionalities for AI-powered testing, from end-to-end testing and UI quality assurance to codeless test automation and visual testing.

AI Tool in Focus: Applitools

Next generation test automation platform powered by Visual AI

Increase quality, accelerate delivery and reduce cost with the world's most intelligent test automation platform.

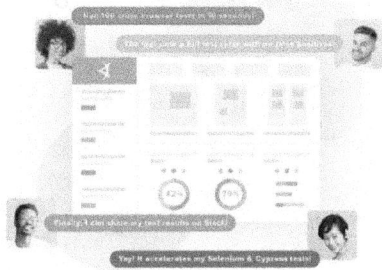

Applitools is an advanced AI-powered test automation platform, specifically designed to enhance software testing with Visual AI technology. Here's a comprehensive overview of its features and capabilities:

1. **Visual AI for Functional and Visual Regression Testing**: Applitools Eyes utilizes Visual AI, a unique computer vision technology that replicates human vision and cognition, to quickly identify both functional and visual regressions. This technology enables the creation of tests that are faster, more stable, and can catch significantly more bugs compared to traditional functional testing methods.

2. **End-to-End Software Testing Platform**: Applitools provides a comprehensive testing platform suitable for various roles within software development, including engineering, test automation, manual QA, DevOps, and digital transformation teams. It is specifically adept at identifying bugs that are often missed by functional tests, including visual bugs.

3. **Codeless Test Creation and Maintenance**: The platform emphasizes reducing manual work throughout the testing process, from test creation to execution. Applitools offers codeless test creation capabilities, meaning tests can be created, maintained, executed, and reported without the need for extensive coding. This feature allows teams to test a vast amount of their application with less effort.

4. **Automated Testing Across Various Aspects**: Applitools' Visual AI enables automation of functional, visual, accessibility, and cross-browser testing, often with just a few lines of code. This capability facilitates rapid feature development and eases the process of updating tests. The platform can integrate with various frameworks, enhancing its adaptability.

5. **Next-Generation Testing Cloud**: The Applitools platform includes tools like the Ultrafast Grid, which allows developers and QA engineers to quickly validate frontend functionality, accessibility, and visual aspects of their applications. This technology helps teams deliver flawless digital experiences efficiently, without the complexities of traditional testing practices.

6. **AI-Powered Auto-Analysis and Maintenance**: Applitools stands out for its AI-powered auto-analysis and auto-maintenance of tests, ensuring high test accuracy and rapid execution. This feature is crucial for maintaining pace with the fast development and deployment cycles in modern software development.

Applitools leverages its proprietary Visual AI technology to offer a robust, efficient, and comprehensive testing platform. Its capabilities in automating and streamlining various aspects of software testing make it a valuable tool for teams aiming to improve their software quality and accelerate their development cycles.

AI in Bug Tracking and Fixing

The integration of Artificial Intelligence (AI) in bug tracking and fixing has marked a revolutionary shift in how software defects are identified, tracked, and resolved. AI algorithms now play a pivotal role in automatically detecting anomalies and potential bugs by analyzing code patterns and user interactions. This automated detection is not only more efficient but also helps in uncovering issues that might be overlooked by traditional methods.

Another significant advancement brought by AI in this field is the prioritization of bugs. AI tools intelligently prioritize bugs based on their impact and severity. This ensures that critical issues are addressed promptly and efficiently, reducing the risk of major software failures or security breaches.

Predictive bug identification is yet another area where AI is making a substantial impact. By analyzing historical data, AI can predict potential bug-ridden areas, enabling software teams to take proactive measures before issues become problematic. This predictive approach helps in maintaining the overall quality and stability of software products.

AI also facilitates a faster resolution of identified bugs. It provides developers with valuable insights and recommendations on how to fix issues, thereby speeding up the resolution process. This assistance is crucial in fast-paced development environments where time is of the essence.

Moreover, AI systems in bug tracking and fixing are designed to continuously learn from each interaction. This learning process improves their capabilities in detecting and resolving bugs over time, making them more efficient and reliable.

In summary, the role of AI in bug tracking and fixing represents a significant advancement in the field of software quality assurance. It offers more efficient and effective ways to maintain and enhance software reliability, thus playing a crucial role in the lifecycle of software development. This technological evolution underscores the increasing importance of AI in addressing complex challenges in software engineering.

Aspect of Bug Tracking and Fixing	Role of AI
Automated Bug Detection	AI algorithms automatically detect anomalies and potential bugs by analyzing code patterns and user interactions.
Prioritization of Bugs	AI tools prioritize bugs based on their impact and severity, focusing attention on critical issues first.
Predictive Bug Identification	By analyzing historical data, AI predicts areas where bugs are likely to occur, enabling proactive measures.
Facilitating Faster Resolution	AI provides insights and recommendations for fixing identified bugs, accelerating the resolution process.
Continuous Learning	AI systems continuously learn from each interaction, improving their bug detection and resolution capabilities over time.

Here is a list of AI tools for bug tracking and fixing, along with their respective URLs:

1. **Bugpilot**: An AI-powered tool for automating bug resolution. Bugpilot.

2. **Bugasura**: An AI-powered bug tracker that streamlines workflows, accelerates bug reporting and resolution, and offers integrations with popular tools. Bugasura.

3. **Codeball**: An AI-powered code review tool that helps find bugs in pull requests and improve code quality. Codeball.

4. **Kodezi**: A code assistant for tasks such as code generation and bug fixes. Kodezi.

5. **Bito**: Offers a suite of coding tools for developers to write and build test cases. Bito.

6. **Codecleaningbot**: A comprehensive code cleaning utility that improves project formatting, security, and customization. Codecleaningbot.

7. **Metabob**: Detects and fixes coding problems using graph neural networks and language models. Metabob.

8. **Codiga**: A static code analysis tool that offers custom analysis rules, secure code analysis, and real-time code analysis and fixes. Codiga.

9. **CodeMate**: Enhances the coding experience by autocorrecting errors, debugging, and providing tailored answers and code review. CodeMate.

10. **Safurai**: An AI Code Assistant (IDE extension) that solves bugs, refactors code, and generates documentation. Safurai.

11. **Explain An Error**: Uses a language model trained on StackExchange to explain code errors and suggest fixes. Explain An Error.

12. **Coderbuds**: An AI-powered code review tool that offers automated reviews and integrates with Github and Slack. Coderbuds.

13. **GitHub Copilot X**: An AI tool that integrates into every part of the software development workflow, offering context-aware conversations and code suggestions. GitHub Copilot X.

Enhancing Software Reliability with AI

AI plays a crucial role in enhancing the reliability of software systems, offering advanced tools and techniques for maintaining and improving software performance.

1. **Predictive Maintenance:**

   - AI algorithms predict potential system failures and software issues, allowing for preventive maintenance and timely interventions.

2. **Real-Time Monitoring and Analysis:**

   - AI-powered monitoring tools continuously analyze software performance, identifying and addressing issues in real-time.

3. **Load Balancing and Resource Management:**

   - AI optimizes resource allocation and load balancing, ensuring software systems operate efficiently under varying workloads.

4. **Adaptive Security Measures:**

   - AI enhances software reliability by implementing adaptive security measures, responding dynamically to potential threats and vulnerabilities.

5. **Self-Healing Systems:**

   - AI enables the development of self-healing systems that automatically detect and correct software faults, minimizing downtime and user disruption.

In summary, AI significantly contributes to software reliability, offering predictive insights, real-time monitoring, efficient resource management, and adaptive security, leading to more robust and dependable software systems.

Here is a list of AI tools that are instrumental in enhancing software reliability, along with their descriptions and URLs:

1. **CodeQL by GitHub**: CodeQL is an AI-powered static analysis tool used by GitHub for automatically identifying security vulnerabilities in code. It not only detects issues but also suggests fixes and patches, contributing significantly to the security of the software ecosystem. CodeQL - GitHub.

2. **Infer by Facebook**: Infer is an AI-based code analysis tool employed by Facebook. It uses static analysis to identify programming errors and potential crashes, even in complex and large-scale codebases, thereby enhancing software reliability and preventing issues from reaching production. Infer - Facebook.

3. **DeepCode by Google**: Developed by Google, DeepCode is an AI-driven code review tool that provides intelligent suggestions for code improvements. It analyzes code patterns, coding styles, and best practices to assist developers in writing cleaner, more efficient code. DeepCode - Google.

4. **Aibolit by Uber**: Aibolit is Uber's AI-based code analysis tool designed to identify code smells, indicators of potential issues in code quality. It assists in maintaining clean and efficient codebases and adhering to coding standards and best practices. Aibolit - Uber.

5. **IntelliCode by Microsoft**: IntelliCode enhances the code review process by offering AI-generated code completion suggestions and recommendations. It analyzes coding patterns and contextual information to assist developers in writing code more efficiently. IntelliCode - Microsoft.

These tools leverage AI to improve various aspects of software reliability, from code analysis and error detection to automated suggestions for code improvements and adherence to best practices.

AI for Project Planning and Risk Assessment

The integration of Artificial Intelligence (AI) into project management, particularly in project planning and risk assessment, is revolutionizing how projects are conceptualized, planned, and executed. AI tools have become instrumental in enhancing the process of project planning. They analyze historical project data, offering valuable insights for planning new projects. These insights include predictions about timelines, resource requirements, and potential bottlenecks, enabling more accurate and efficient project planning.

In the realm of risk prediction and mitigation, AI algorithms play a critical role. They identify potential risks by analyzing patterns from past projects and current market trends. This capability of early risk identification allows project managers to develop proactive mitigation strategies, significantly reducing potential project setbacks.

Another area where AI greatly contributes is in the optimization of resource allocation. AI systems assist in the optimal distribution of resources, including personnel and budget, by considering the project's requirements and individual skill sets. This ensures the effective and efficient use of resources, which is crucial for the success of any project.

AI tools are also adept at dynamically adapting project plans in response to changes. Whether these changes are in scope, resources, or external factors, AI helps maintain the project's alignment with its objectives. This dynamic adaptation is essential in today's fast-paced and often unpredictable project environments.

Predictive analytics powered by AI are invaluable in decision-making processes. These analytics aid project managers in foreseeing the outcomes of different choices, guiding them in selecting the best course of action. This foresight is particularly beneficial in complex project scenarios where each decision can significantly impact the project's outcome.

In summary, AI plays a crucial role in project planning and risk assessment. Its ability to enhance the efficiency, accuracy, and success rate of projects is invaluable. By leveraging AI, organizations can better navigate the complexities of project management, leading to more predictable and favorable outcomes. This technological advancement is transforming the landscape of project management, making it more data-driven and effective.

Here is a list of AI project management tools that can assist in project planning and risk assessment, along with their URLs:

1. **Trello**: Known for its affordable pricing and intuitive project management capabilities. Visit Trello.

2. **ClickUp**: Best for customizations, offering a flexible and feature-rich project management solution. Visit ClickUp.

3. **Notion**: Notable for providing writing assistance, useful in managing project documentation. Visit Notion.

4. **Wrike**: Offers unique AI features to enhance project management tasks. Visit Wrike.

5. **Asana**: Includes AI features for streamlining project management processes. Visit Asana.

6. **monday.com**: Suitable for teams of most sizes, with AI features to optimize project management. Visit monday.com.

7. **Microsoft Project**: Ideal for Microsoft 365 users, integrating AI features into project management. Visit Microsoft Project.

These tools offer a range of AI-driven functionalities to enhance project planning, risk assessment, and overall project management efficiency.

AI Tool in Focus: Notion

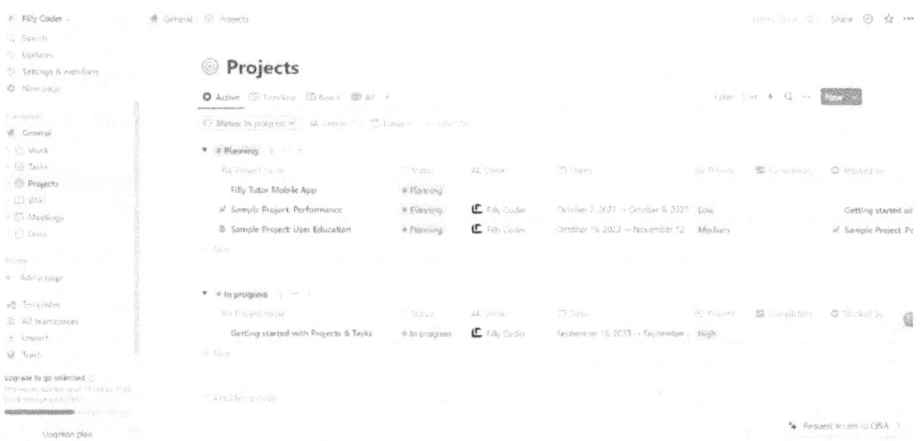

Notion is a versatile productivity and organization tool designed to streamline workflows for individuals and teams. It's not directly an AI tool, but it incorporates various technological features that enhance user experience and efficiency. Key aspects of Notion include:

1. **All-in-One Workspace**: Notion serves as a unified workspace for notes, tasks, wikis, and databases. It allows users to create custom pages that can contain text, images, bookmarks, code snippets, and other types of content.

2. **Customization and Flexibility**: One of Notion's standout features is its high level of customization. Users can tailor the tool to their specific needs, whether it's for personal use, project management, or team collaboration. This includes creating templates for various purposes like task management, note-taking, project tracking, and more.

3. **Collaboration Features**: Notion facilitates team collaboration by allowing multiple users to work on the same page simultaneously. It offers features like comments, mentions, and shared workspaces, making it suitable for team projects, content creation, and knowledge sharing.

4. **Integration Capabilities**: It integrates with various other tools and platforms, enhancing its functionality and enabling users to connect their workflows with other applications they use.

5. **Database Functionality**: Notion's database feature is particularly powerful, allowing users to create and manage tables, kanban boards, calendars, and lists. These databases can be customized with different views and properties, making them useful for a wide range of applications, from CRM to content calendars.

6. **Templates and Community**: The platform provides a wide range of templates for different use cases, contributed by both Notion and its user community. This vast library of templates enables new users to quickly start with pre-designed layouts and structures.

7. **Mobile and Web Access**: Notion is accessible via web browsers and offers mobile applications for iOS and Android, allowing users to stay connected and productive across devices.

8. **Subscription Model**: While Notion offers a free tier with basic features, it also has paid plans that provide additional functionality and resources. These plans cater to individuals, teams, and enterprises with varying needs and scales.

Notion is widely praised for its clean interface, flexibility, and powerful organizational capabilities, making it a popular choice among productivity enthusiasts, teams, and companies looking to centralize their workflows and information management.

AI Tools for Team Collaboration and Communication

In the rapidly evolving digital workplace, AI tools have become indispensable for enhancing team collaboration and communication. These tools not only streamline workflows but also foster a more connected and efficient work environment. Below, we explore some of the key AI tools that are transforming the way teams interact and work together.

1. AI-Powered Chatbots and Virtual Assistants

*   **Functionality**: These AI-driven programs can handle routine inquiries, schedule meetings, and even provide project updates, freeing up human resources for more complex tasks.

*   **Examples**: Slackbot in Slack, which assists in automating responses and tasks, and Microsoft's Cortana, which integrates with Microsoft 365 for scheduling and reminders.

2. Intelligent Communication Platforms

*   **Overview**: Platforms like Microsoft Teams and Slack use AI to analyze communication patterns, suggest relevant documents, and even recommend experts within the organization for specific queries.

- **Benefits**: They reduce the time spent searching for information and connect team members more efficiently.

3. **Project Management Tools with AI**

- **Capabilities**: AI in project management tools can predict project timelines, allocate resources effectively, and identify potential bottlenecks before they become issues.

- **Examples**: Trello and Asana, which use AI to automate task assignments based on workload and expertise.

4. **AI-Enhanced Collaboration Tools**

- **Functionality**: Tools like Google Workspace and Microsoft 365 use AI to offer real-time collaboration, smart suggestions, and predictive text, enhancing the quality of collaborative work.

- **Advantages**: These features save time and improve the accuracy of collaborative documents.

5. **Sentiment Analysis and Employee Engagement Tools**

- **Purpose**: AI tools can analyze communication patterns to gauge team morale and employee engagement, providing insights into the team's health.

- **Examples**: Tools like Culture Amp and Glint use AI to analyze survey responses and provide actionable insights.

6. **Automated Transcription and Meeting Summaries**

- **Use Case**: AI-driven transcription services like Otter.ai transcribe meetings in real-time, providing accessible records and summaries for those who couldn't attend.

- **Benefits**: This ensures all team members are on the same page and can reference discussions easily.

7. **Language Translation Tools**

- **Importance**: For global teams, AI-powered translation tools are essential for overcoming language barriers in real-time communication.

- **Examples**: Google Translate and Microsoft Translator integrate with various communication platforms to provide seamless translation.

8. **Custom AI Solutions**

- **Tailored Tools**: Some organizations develop custom AI solutions tailored to their specific communication and collaboration needs, often integrating with existing tools for a seamless experience.

9. **Security and Compliance**

- **AI Role**: AI tools also play a crucial role in ensuring communication and collaboration tools adhere to security protocols and compliance requirements, detecting anomalies and potential threats.

10. **Future Trends**

- **Emerging Technologies**: The integration of augmented reality (AR) and virtual reality (VR) in collaboration tools, offering more immersive and interactive meeting experiences.

AI tools for team collaboration and communication are not just about efficiency; they are about creating a more connected, creative, and adaptable workforce. As these tools evolve, they promise to further revolutionize the way teams work together in the digital age.

Here's a list of AI tools designed for team collaboration and communication, along with their URLs:

1. **Slackbot in Slack**

    - **Description**: An AI-powered chatbot within Slack that can automate responses and tasks.

    - **URL**: Slackbot

2. **Microsoft Cortana**

    - **Description**: Integrated with Microsoft 365, Cortana assists in scheduling, reminders, and email management.

    - **URL**: Microsoft Cortana

3. **Microsoft Teams**

    - **Description**: Uses AI to analyze communication patterns and suggest relevant documents or experts.

    - **URL**: Microsoft Teams

4. **Trello**

    - **Description**: A project management tool that uses AI for automating task assignments and project planning.

    - **URL**: Trello

5. **Asana**

    - **Description**: Features AI capabilities for task management and workload balancing.

    - **URL**: Asana

6. **Google Workspace**

   - **Description**: Offers AI-driven real-time collaboration, smart suggestions, and predictive text.

   - **URL**: Google Workspace

7. **Culture Amp**

   - **Description**: Utilizes AI for employee engagement and performance analysis.

   - **URL**: Culture Amp

8. **Glint**

   - **Description**: An AI tool for analyzing team engagement and morale through surveys.

   - **URL**: Glint

9. **Otter.ai**

   - **Description**: Provides AI-driven transcription services for meetings and events.

   - **URL**: Otter.ai

10. **Google Translate**

    - **Description**: AI-powered language translation tool for real-time communication.

    - **URL**: Google Translate

11. **Microsoft Translator**

    - **Description**: Offers real-time translation for global team communication.

    - **URL**: Microsoft Translator

Each of these tools offers unique features that can significantly enhance team collaboration and communication, leveraging the power of AI to streamline processes and improve efficiency.

AI Tool in Focus: Trello

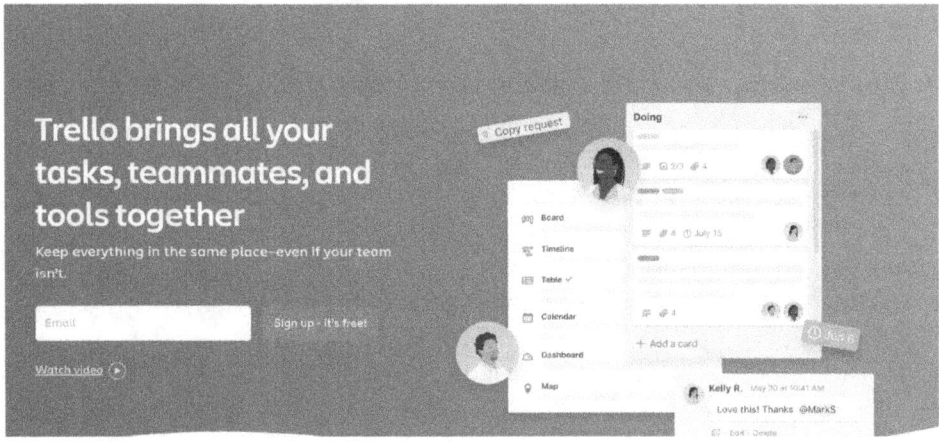

Trello is a popular web-based project management application that utilizes the Kanban board approach for organizing tasks and workflows. Here are some key features and aspects of Trello:

1. **Kanban Boards**: At its core, Trello uses boards, lists, and cards to help users organize and prioritize projects in a flexible, visual, and collaborative way. Each board represents a project or workflow, lists within boards represent stages or categories, and cards are used for tasks or items.

2. **Collaboration**: Trello is designed to facilitate team collaboration. Multiple users can work on the same board, add comments to cards, attach files, and assign tasks. It supports real-time updates, ensuring all team members see the most current version of a board.

3. **Customization and Flexibility**: Users can customize boards, lists, and cards to fit their specific project needs. Trello offers various power-ups (add-ons) that extend its functionality, such as adding calendar views, voting on cards, or integrating with other applications like Slack, Google Drive, and more.

4. **Ease of Use**: Trello is known for its user-friendly interface and simplicity. Its drag-and-drop functionality makes it easy to move cards across lists as tasks progress. This intuitive design makes it accessible for users with varying levels of technical proficiency.

5. **Notifications and Automation**: Trello keeps users informed through notifications about task updates, due dates, and mentions. It also offers automation features through 'Butler', which automates common tasks like moving cards, creating lists, or sending reminders.

6. **Templates**: Trello provides a variety of templates for different use cases, such as business, education, and personal productivity. These templates give users a head start in setting up their boards.

7. **Mobile Accessibility**: Trello offers mobile applications for iOS and Android, allowing users to access their boards and manage tasks on-the-go.

8. **Subscription Tiers**: While Trello offers a free version with basic features, it also has premium plans (Trello Gold, Business Class, and Enterprise) that offer additional capabilities, more power-ups, larger file attachments, and advanced features for larger teams or organizations.

Trello is widely used in various contexts, from managing simple personal tasks to complex project management in businesses. Its visual approach to task management and emphasis on collaboration make it a popular choice among teams looking to improve their productivity and workflow management.

Predictive Analytics in Project Management

Predictive analytics is revolutionizing project management by providing insights that help in making informed decisions, anticipating problems, and improving outcomes. This section delves into how predictive analytics is being utilized in project management, its benefits, challenges, and future prospects.

1. **Understanding Predictive Analytics in Project Management**

   - **Definition**: Predictive analytics involves using historical data, statistical algorithms, and machine learning techniques to identify the likelihood of future outcomes.

   - **Application**: In project management, it's used to forecast project risks, schedule delays, cost overruns, and other critical aspects.

2. **Key Benefits**

   - **Risk Mitigation**: By predicting potential issues, teams can proactively address risks before they impact the project.

   - **Resource Optimization**: Predictive analytics helps in efficient allocation of resources, ensuring that they are used where they are most needed.

   - **Improved Decision Making**: Data-driven insights aid in making more informed decisions, reducing the reliance on guesswork or intuition.

3. **Data Sources and Integration**

   - **Data Collection**: Data from various sources like past project records, team performance data, and external factors are collected.

   - **Integration**: This data is then integrated into project management tools to provide a comprehensive view of the project landscape.

4. **Techniques and Tools**

   - **Statistical Methods**: Techniques like regression analysis, time series analysis, and probability models are commonly used.

   - **AI and Machine Learning**: Advanced tools employ machine learning algorithms to improve the accuracy of predictions over time.

- **Software Examples**: Tools like Microsoft Project, JIRA with predictive plugins, and specialized software like RiskyProject.

5. Applications in Project Management

- **Schedule Predictions**: Forecasting project timelines and identifying potential delays.

- **Budget Forecasts**: Estimating costs and predicting overruns.

- **Quality Control**: Anticipating quality issues based on historical data.

- **Performance Analysis**: Evaluating team and individual performance trends to predict future productivity.

6. Challenges and Limitations

- **Data Quality and Quantity**: The accuracy of predictions depends on the quality and quantity of available data.

- **Complexity and Expertise**: Implementing predictive analytics requires a certain level of expertise and understanding of statistical models.

- **Change Management**: Integrating predictive analytics into existing project management processes can be challenging.

7. Ethical Considerations and Privacy

- **Data Privacy**: Ensuring the privacy and security of sensitive project data.

- **Ethical Use**: Using predictive analytics ethically, especially when it comes to personnel-related predictions.

8. Future Trends and Developments

- **Integration with IoT and Big Data**: Leveraging IoT for real-time data collection and big data for more comprehensive analysis.

- **Enhanced AI Capabilities**: Improved machine learning models for more accurate and nuanced predictions.

- **Predictive Analytics as a Standard**: Becoming a standard feature in project management software and methodologies.

Predictive analytics is transforming project management from a reactive discipline into a proactive one. By leveraging data and advanced analytics, project managers can foresee challenges and opportunities, leading to more successful project outcomes. As technology advances, the role of predictive analytics in project management is set to become even more pivotal.

Here is a list of AI tools for project management, specifically useful for predictive analytics and risk assessment, along with their key features:

1. **Asana**: A popular tool that integrates AI features to enhance team collaboration, task management, and project tracking. It provides a user-friendly interface and a comprehensive set of features for various project management needs. Asana Intelligence.

2. **Monday.com**: Incorporates AI to streamline team coordination and automate routine tasks. Its user-friendly interface allows teams to plan, track, and manage projects effortlessly. Monday AI.

3. **Trello**: Known for its simplicity and ease of use, Trello integrates AI capabilities to enhance productivity and streamline task management. Its AI-driven smart suggestions help in task assignments, due dates, and managing task dependencies. Trello Power-Ups.

4. **ClickUp**: A comprehensive project management platform integrating AI features to simplify complex projects. It provides insights on task prioritization, resource allocation, and project timelines, adapting to individual work styles for optimizing productivity. ClickUp AI.

5. **Microsoft Project**: A widely recognized project management software that incorporates AI features to enhance project planning, scheduling, and resource management. It provides effective tools for planning, executing, and tracking projects. Microsoft Project.

6. **Wrike**: Combines task management, collaboration, and project tracking functionalities. While not heavily focused on native AI capabilities, Wrike integrates with AI-powered solutions to enhance its features. Wrike Lightspeed.

These tools offer a range of AI-powered features to assist in predictive analytics, risk assessment, and overall project management, enhancing efficiency and decision-making processes.

Chapter 7: AI in Deployment and Maintenance

AI in Continuous Integration and Deployment (CI/CD)

The integration of Artificial Intelligence (AI) in Continuous Integration and Continuous Deployment (CI/CD) pipelines represents a significant leap in software development and operational processes. This section explores how AI is transforming CI/CD, making it more efficient, predictive, and adaptive.

1. **Overview of AI in CI/CD**

   - **Definition**: AI in CI/CD involves the use of machine learning algorithms and data analytics to automate, optimize, and enhance software development and deployment processes.

   - **Purpose**: The goal is to reduce manual effort, minimize errors, predict potential issues, and streamline the entire software release cycle.

2. **AI-Driven Code Integration and Testing**

   - **Automated Code Reviews**: AI tools can analyze code commits for quality assurance, coding standards, and security vulnerabilities.

   - **Predictive Test Selection**: AI algorithms predict which tests are most relevant based on code changes, reducing test cycle time.

   - **Flaky Test Identification**: AI identifies and isolates flaky tests – tests that exhibit inconsistent results – improving the reliability of the testing suite.

3. **Enhanced Deployment Strategies**

   - **Predictive Deployment Models**: AI models predict the success of deployments based on historical data, helping in risk assessment and mitigation strategies.

   - **Automated Canary Releases**: AI systems can manage canary releases, gradually rolling out changes to a small subset of users and scaling up based on real-time feedback and performance metrics.

4. **Performance Optimization and Monitoring**

   - **Real-time Monitoring**: AI tools provide real-time monitoring of applications, identifying performance issues and anomalies.

   - **Predictive Analytics**: Using predictive analytics, AI can forecast potential system downtimes or performance degradations, allowing preemptive action.

5. **Feedback Loop and Learning**

   - **Continuous Learning**: AI systems continuously learn from each deployment, integrating feedback into future CI/CD cycles.

   - **Feedback Analysis**: AI analyzes feedback from various stages of the CI/CD pipeline, including development, testing, deployment, and production, to enhance process efficiency.

6. **Challenges and Considerations**

   - **Data Quality and Quantity**: The effectiveness of AI in CI/CD is heavily dependent on the quality and quantity of data from software development processes.

- **Integration Complexity**: Integrating AI into existing CI/CD pipelines can be complex and requires careful planning and execution.

- **Skill Requirements**: There is a need for skills in both AI and software engineering to effectively implement AI in CI/CD.

7. Future Prospects

- **Advanced Predictive Models**: Future developments may include more sophisticated AI models capable of handling complex deployment scenarios and predicting outcomes with higher accuracy.

- **AI-Driven Development Environments**: The integration of AI into development environments, providing real-time assistance and recommendations to developers.

The incorporation of AI into CI/CD pipelines is a game-changer in software development and deployment. It not only automates and optimizes processes but also brings a level of predictive intelligence that can significantly reduce time-to-market, enhance software quality, and improve overall operational efficiency. As AI technology continues to evolve, its role in CI/CD is expected to become more integral and transformative.

AI Tool in Focus: Snyk

Snyk is a powerful tool that uses AI to enhance code security and developer productivity. Here are some of its key features:

1. **DeepCode AI Knowledge Base**: Snyk employs a unique process to create the DeepCode AI knowledge base for powering Snyk Code. This involves a combination of symbolic and

generative AI, several machine learning methods, and the expertise of Snyk security researchers, ensuring high accuracy and efficiency in detecting vulnerabilities and offering AI-powered fixes.

2. **Real-Time Code Scanning and Vulnerability Fixes**: Snyk integrates with the development environment, scanning code in real-time as it's written and updated. It flags vulnerabilities directly in the IDE and offers recommendations for fixes, which developers can apply with a click. This real-time scanning and fixing mechanism significantly enhances code security and streamlines the development process.

3. **Developer-First Static Application Security Testing (SAST)**: Snyk Code is designed to augment the developer experience with its unrivaled speed and accuracy. This AI-powered approach leads to more efficient teams and secure products, as it empowers and motivates developers by increasing code security and offering an intuitive platform for security analysis and fixes.

4. **Hybrid AI Approach**: Snyk utilizes a hybrid AI approach, combining machine learning (ML), symbolic AI, and human intelligence. This comprehensive approach allows Snyk to focus on providing and perfecting service quality and accuracy in security research, predominantly behind the scenes.

Overall, Snyk stands out as a tool that not only enhances security in the coding process but also contributes to increased developer productivity and code quality. It addresses the crucial need for security in modern software development, especially in environments where rapid code generation and deployment are common.

For more information, you can visit Snyk's website:

- Snyk DeepCode AI

- Snyk Code Security Analysis

Here's a list of AI tools that are relevant to continuous integration and deployment (CI/CD), along with their URLs:

1. **Kite**

    - **Description**: An AI-powered coding assistant that helps developers write code faster with less effort. It integrates with popular development environments to provide intelligent code completions.

    - **URL**: Kite

2. **DeepCode**

    - **Description**: This tool uses AI to review code and provide insights. It can detect security vulnerabilities, performance issues, and bad coding practices.

    - **URL**: DeepCode

3. **Code Climate**

    - **Description**: An automated code review tool that uses AI to analyze and improve code quality. It integrates with GitHub and provides real-time feedback.

    - **URL**: Code Climate

4. **LaunchDarkly**

    - **Description**: An AI-powered feature management platform that enables teams to control feature releases, perform canary launches, and analyze the impact of new features.

    - **URL**: LaunchDarkly

5. **Datadog**

    - **Description**: Provides monitoring services for cloud-scale applications, including real-time performance tracking and predictive analytics.

    - **URL**: Datadog

6. **Dynatrace**

    - **Description**: An AI-powered, automated performance monitoring tool. It offers full-stack monitoring, from applications to infrastructure, and uses AI to detect and diagnose complex issues.

    - **URL**: Dynatrace

7. **New Relic**

    - **Description**: Offers AI-powered full-stack monitoring, from applications to servers, and provides insights for better performance optimization.

    - **URL**: New Relic

8. **GitLab**

    - **Description**: While primarily known as a DevOps platform, GitLab incorporates AI in various aspects of its CI/CD pipeline, such as automated code review and issue triaging.

    - **URL**: GitLab

9. **Jenkins X**

    - **Description**: An open-source CI/CD solution for modern cloud applications on Kubernetes. Jenkins X uses AI for various aspects of pipeline optimization and error diagnosis.

    - **URL**: Jenkins X

10. **CircleCI**

- **Description**: A CI/CD tool that integrates with GitHub and Bitbucket. It uses AI for intelligent caching, test splitting, and insights to improve build times and efficiency.

- **URL**: CircleCI

Each of these tools brings unique AI-driven capabilities to the CI/CD process, enhancing efficiency, accuracy, and overall software quality. They represent the forefront of integrating AI into software development and operational workflows.

AI for Real-Time Monitoring and Maintenance

In an era where uninterrupted performance of systems and infrastructure is critical to business operations, Artificial Intelligence (AI) has emerged as a game-changer in real-time monitoring and maintenance. This technological advancement offers proactive solutions to detect, predict, and address issues before they impact operations, transforming the way businesses handle system and infrastructure maintenance.

The significance of real-time monitoring cannot be overstated, particularly in mission-critical systems found in industries like finance, healthcare, and manufacturing, where downtime is not an option. Additionally, the explosion of data in today's digital world necessitates constant vigilance to ensure data integrity and availability. This constant monitoring is also crucial for maintaining the seamless customer experiences expected in the digital age.

AI-powered monitoring systems bring a new level of intelligence to these operations. They can analyze vast amounts of data and generate alerts for anomalies or issues, and their machine learning models can predict potential failures based on historical data. This predictive capability allows for proactive maintenance, which is invaluable in avoiding system failures.

The applications of AI in real-time monitoring and maintenance are diverse. In the Industrial Internet of Things (IIoT), AI-driven sensors and devices monitor machinery in manufacturing settings, predicting breakdowns and optimizing maintenance schedules. In IT infrastructure monitoring, AI tools track server performance, network health, and cybersecurity threats in real time. AI also plays a significant role in energy management in smart buildings and predictive healthcare, where it can predict patient deterioration and equipment failures.

However, there are challenges and considerations in implementing AI for real-time monitoring. The effectiveness of these AI systems depends on the quality and accuracy of the data they receive. Integrating AI into existing monitoring systems can be complex and requires careful planning. Additionally, the AI systems themselves need robust security measures to prevent tampering or exploitation.

The benefits of AI-driven real-time monitoring are numerous. They include reduced downtime due to predictive maintenance, cost savings from proactive rather than reactive maintenance, and enhanced system performance, leading to improved productivity and customer satisfaction.

Looking ahead, future trends and developments in AI for real-time monitoring are promising. Edge computing will allow AI algorithms to run on edge devices, enabling faster responses and reduced data transfer latency. AI will also play a vital role in enhancing cybersecurity and developing fully autonomous systems that perform maintenance tasks without human intervention.

In conclusion, AI-driven real-time monitoring and maintenance represent a paradigm shift from reactive to proactive approaches in system management. Organizations that embrace AI in this domain gain a competitive advantage by ensuring reliability, efficiency, and customer satisfaction. As AI technology continues to evolve, its role in detecting, predicting, and responding to issues in real time will become increasingly sophisticated and essential for businesses and industries globally.

Here's a list of AI tools and platforms relevant to real-time monitoring and maintenance, along with their URLs:

1. **Splunk**

    - **Description**: Splunk uses AI and machine learning for real-time log analysis, monitoring, and alerting to help organizations detect and resolve issues quickly.

    - **URL**: Splunk

2. **AppDynamics**

    - **Description**: AppDynamics provides AI-powered application performance monitoring and real-time insights to optimize application performance and reliability.

    - **URL**: AppDynamics

3. **Nagios XI**

    - **Description**: Nagios XI offers AI-driven monitoring and alerting for IT infrastructure, including servers, networks, and applications.

    - **URL**: Nagios XI

4. **Datadog**

    - **Description**: Datadog offers AI-driven monitoring and analytics for cloud-scale applications, providing real-time insights into system performance.

    - **URL**: Datadog

5. **Dynatrace**

    - **Description**: Dynatrace is an AI-powered observability platform that offers real-time monitoring and automation for cloud-native applications.

- **URL**: Dynatrace

6. **LogicMonitor**

   - **Description**: LogicMonitor uses AI for infrastructure and application monitoring, providing real-time visibility and predictive insights.

   - **URL**: LogicMonitor

7. **PRTG Network Monitor**

   - **Description**: PRTG Network Monitor includes AI-driven features for network and infrastructure monitoring, helping identify and resolve issues in real time.

   - **URL**: PRTG Network Monitor

8. **SolarWinds**

   - **Description**: SolarWinds offers AI-based solutions for network, infrastructure, and application performance monitoring.

   - **URL**: SolarWinds

9. **OpsRamp**

   - **Description**: OpsRamp provides AI-driven IT operations management, enabling real-time monitoring and incident management.

   - **URL**: OpsRamp

10. **IBM Watson AIOps**

    - **Description**: IBM Watson AIOps uses AI to automate incident resolution, optimize operations, and provide real-time insights for IT environments.

    - **URL**: IBM Watson AIOps

These AI tools and platforms empower organizations to monitor their systems, infrastructure, and applications in real time, detect anomalies, predict issues, and take proactive maintenance actions. They play a crucial role in ensuring the reliability and performance of critical IT systems.

Predictive Maintenance Using AI

Predictive maintenance, powered by Artificial Intelligence (AI), is revolutionizing industries by shifting from traditional, reactive maintenance strategies to proactive, data-driven approaches. This section explores how AI is transforming maintenance practices across various sectors, enhancing equipment reliability, and reducing downtime.

1. **The Need for Predictive Maintenance**

- **Downtime Costs**: Unscheduled downtime can incur significant financial losses, especially in industries reliant on continuous operation.

- **Asset Health**: Aging equipment requires precise monitoring to maintain performance and safety.

- **Operational Efficiency**: Predictive maintenance optimizes maintenance schedules, reducing over-maintenance and under-maintenance scenarios.

2. **How AI Powers Predictive Maintenance**

- **Sensor Data**: AI systems analyze sensor data, such as temperature, vibration, and pressure, to detect anomalies.

- **Machine Learning Algorithms**: Algorithms learn from historical data to predict equipment failures or degradation.

- **Prescriptive Analysis**: AI provides recommendations for maintenance actions, including timing and type.

3. **Applications Across Industries**

- **Manufacturing**: Predictive maintenance prevents unexpected machine breakdowns, optimizing production efficiency.

- **Aviation**: Airlines use AI to predict aircraft component failures, ensuring passenger safety and on-time flights.

- **Energy**: Power plants employ predictive maintenance to prevent costly turbine failures and optimize energy production.

- **Transportation**: AI monitors vehicle health in real-time, reducing maintenance costs and improving safety.

4. **Benefits of Predictive Maintenance**

- **Cost Reduction**: Proactive maintenance minimizes unscheduled downtime, saving costs associated with repairs and lost production.

- **Improved Safety**: Early detection of equipment issues enhances workplace safety and reduces the risk of accidents.

- **Asset Longevity**: Equipment life expectancy increases, reducing the need for premature replacements.

5. **Challenges and Considerations**

- **Data Quality**: Accurate sensor data and historical records are crucial for AI-driven predictions.

- **Integration**: Implementing AI into existing systems and workflows requires planning and integration efforts.

- **Change Management**: Employees need training to adapt to the new predictive maintenance processes.

6. Future Trends and Developments

- **Edge AI**: Edge computing and AI enable real-time analysis of sensor data directly at the source, reducing latency.

- **Digital Twins**: AI-driven digital twins create virtual replicas of physical assets for more accurate predictions and simulations.

- **Predictive Analytics Platforms**: Specialized platforms continue to emerge, simplifying the adoption of predictive maintenance.

7. Conclusion

- **Transformative Impact**: AI-driven predictive maintenance is a transformative shift from reactive to proactive maintenance practices.

- **Competitive Advantage**: Organizations embracing AI for predictive maintenance gain a competitive edge by reducing downtime, enhancing reliability, and optimizing costs.

Predictive maintenance using AI is no longer a luxury but a necessity for industries aiming to stay competitive and efficient in today's rapidly changing world. As AI technologies continue to evolve, the accuracy and sophistication of predictive maintenance systems will only increase, further improving asset reliability and operational excellence.

Here's a list of AI tools and platforms relevant to predictive maintenance, along with their URLs:

1. **IBM Maximo**

   - **Description**: IBM Maximo Asset Monitor uses AI and IoT data to predict equipment failures and optimize maintenance schedules.

   - **URL**: IBM Maximo

2. **SAP Predictive Maintenance and Service**

   - **Description**: SAP's solution leverages AI and machine learning to monitor equipment and predict maintenance needs.

   - **URL**: SAP Predictive Maintenance and Service

3. **Microsoft Azure IoT**

   - **Description**: Azure IoT offers tools and services for predictive maintenance, including machine learning capabilities for analyzing sensor data.

   - **URL**: Microsoft Azure IoT

4. **Predix by GE Digital**

   - **Description**: Predix is an industrial IoT platform that uses AI to optimize asset performance and enable predictive maintenance.

   - **URL**: Predix

5. **Uptake**

   - **Description**: Uptake provides AI-driven predictive analytics for asset-intensive industries, offering insights into equipment health and maintenance needs.

   - **URL**: Uptake

6. **C3 AI**

   - **Description**: C3 AI offers a suite of AI applications, including predictive maintenance, to improve asset reliability and performance.

   - **URL**: C3 AI

7. **PTC ThingWorx**

   - **Description**: ThingWorx is an IoT platform that includes predictive maintenance features for monitoring and optimizing assets.

   - **URL**: PTC ThingWorx

8. **Bosch IoT Suite**

   - **Description**: Bosch IoT Suite provides AI-powered predictive maintenance solutions for various industries.

   - **URL**: Bosch IoT Suite

9. **Senseye**

   - **Description**: Senseye offers AI-based predictive maintenance for manufacturing and industrial operations.

   - **URL**: Senseye

10. **Augury**

    - **Description**: Augury provides AI-driven insights into industrial equipment health, offering predictive maintenance solutions.

    - **URL**: Augury

These AI tools and platforms empower organizations to implement predictive maintenance strategies, utilizing AI and machine learning to monitor equipment health, predict failures, and optimize maintenance schedules. They play a crucial role in minimizing downtime, reducing maintenance costs, and improving overall operational efficiency.

Chapter 8: AI in Security

AI in Cybersecurity and Threat Detection

In the rapidly evolving landscape of cybersecurity, Artificial Intelligence (AI) has emerged as a powerful ally in safeguarding digital assets and sensitive information. This section delves into how AI is reshaping the field of cybersecurity, bolstering threat detection, and enhancing defense mechanisms.

1. **The Evolving Cyber Threat Landscape**

   - **Sophistication of Attacks**: Cyberattacks are becoming increasingly sophisticated, with attackers continuously adapting their methods.

   - **Volume and Velocity**: The sheer volume of data and the speed at which threats emerge require intelligent, automated responses.

   - **Human Limitations**: Human analysts alone cannot keep pace with the scale and complexity of modern threats.

2. **How AI Reinforces Cybersecurity**

   - **Behavioral Analytics**: AI algorithms analyze user and system behavior to identify anomalies indicative of potential threats.

   - **Pattern Recognition**: Machine learning models detect patterns and trends in data that may indicate a cyberattack in progress.

   - **Real-time Monitoring**: AI systems provide continuous real-time monitoring for immediate threat identification and response.

3. **Applications in Cybersecurity**

   - **Intrusion Detection**: AI helps in identifying unauthorized access and abnormal activities within networks.

   - **Malware Detection**: AI-powered antivirus solutions can detect and mitigate malware in real time.

   - **Phishing Detection**: Machine learning models analyze email content to identify phishing attempts.

   - **Zero-Day Vulnerability Identification**: AI can proactively identify and patch vulnerabilities before they are exploited.

4. **Benefits of AI in Cybersecurity**

   - **Proactive Defense**: AI enables organizations to move from reactive to proactive cybersecurity strategies, reducing response times.

   - **Reduced False Positives**: Advanced AI algorithms minimize false positives, ensuring efficient resource allocation.

- **Scalability**: AI can scale effortlessly to handle vast amounts of data and devices, making it suitable for modern, interconnected environments.

5. Challenges and Considerations

- **Adversarial AI**: Attackers may also employ AI to evade detection, leading to an ongoing AI arms race in cybersecurity.

- **Data Privacy**: The use of AI in cybersecurity raises concerns about the privacy of sensitive data.

- **Human Oversight**: While AI is powerful, human expertise remains essential in interpreting results and making strategic decisions.

6. Future Trends and Developments

- **AI-Powered Autonomous Security**: AI systems will autonomously respond to threats without human intervention.

- **Federated Learning**: Collaborative AI models will share threat intelligence while preserving data privacy.

- **AI in IoT Security**: As the Internet of Things (IoT) grows, AI will play a vital role in securing IoT devices.

7. Conclusion

- **Cybersecurity Imperative**: AI is no longer an option but a necessity in safeguarding digital assets and maintaining the integrity of data.

- **Constant Evolution**: As cyber threats evolve, so must AI-driven security solutions, ensuring organizations stay one step ahead of attackers.

Artificial Intelligence has become a cornerstone in the fight against cyber threats. Its ability to analyze vast datasets, identify anomalies, and respond in real time makes it an invaluable asset in the modern cybersecurity arsenal. As AI technology continues to mature, its role in safeguarding digital ecosystems will become increasingly crucial.

AI Tool in Focus: Darktrace

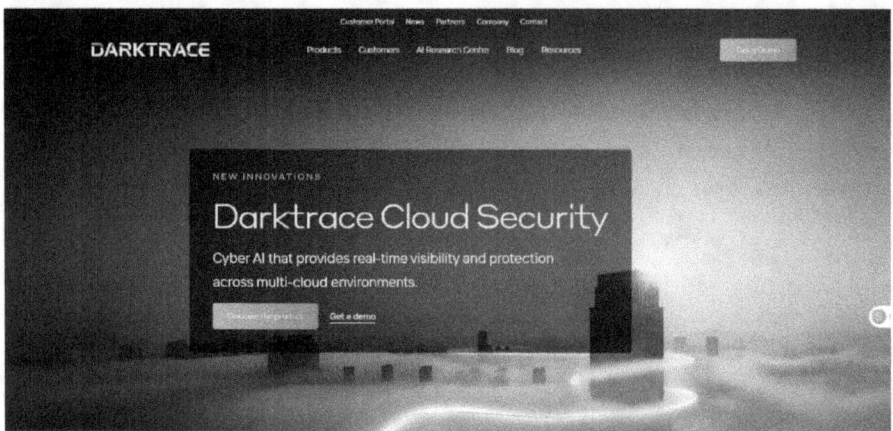

Darktrace is a leading cybersecurity company known for its innovative use of artificial intelligence (AI) to protect networks and digital systems from threats. Here are some key aspects of Darktrace:

1. **Foundation and Growth**: Darktrace was founded in 2013 in Cambridge, UK. Since its inception, the company has grown significantly and is recognized globally for its advanced cyber defense solutions.

2. **Core Technology**: The cornerstone of Darktrace's technology is its AI algorithms, which are designed to detect and respond to cyber threats in real-time. The AI system, inspired by the human immune system, learns and understands the 'pattern of life' for every user and device in an organization's network. This enables it to detect anomalies that may indicate a cyber threat.

3. **Enterprise Immune System**: One of Darktrace's flagship products is the "Enterprise Immune System." This tool uses machine learning and AI to detect, respond, and mitigate cyber threats across diverse digital environments, including cloud services, IoT devices, and traditional networks.

4. **Antigena Module**: Darktrace also offers the Antigena module, which acts as an automated response solution. It can take precise actions to counteract in-progress cyber-threats in real-time, reducing the workload on cybersecurity teams and mitigating risks more efficiently.

5. **Cyber AI Analyst**: Darktrace's Cyber AI Analyst technology automates threat investigations, emulating human thought processes to reduce the time and resources needed for threat analysis.

6. **Applications Across Industries**: Darktrace's solutions are used across various industries, including finance, healthcare, and government, highlighting its versatility in different digital environments.

7. **Awards and Recognition**: The company has received numerous awards for its innovative technology and has been recognized as a leader in AI-driven cybersecurity solutions.

8. **Global Presence**: Darktrace operates globally, with offices in various countries. This wide presence allows the company to cater to a diverse range of clients and adapt to different cybersecurity challenges worldwide.

9. **Stock Market Listing**: Darktrace went public in April 2021, listing on the London Stock Exchange. Its IPO was a significant event in the tech industry, reflecting the growing importance of AI in cybersecurity.

Darktrace's approach to cybersecurity, leveraging AI and machine learning, represents a shift from traditional, rule-based security systems to more adaptive and proactive solutions. This positions the company at the forefront of the fight against increasingly sophisticated cyber threats.

Here's a list of AI tools and platforms relevant to cybersecurity and threat detection.

Darktrace

- **Description**: Darktrace uses AI for cyber defense, employing machine learning to detect and respond to threats in real time.

- **URL**: Darktrace

2. **CrowdStrike**

- **Description**: CrowdStrike's Falcon platform uses AI to provide endpoint security, threat intelligence, and incident response.

- **URL**: CrowdStrike

3. **CylancePROTECT**

- **Description**: CylancePROTECT is an AI-driven antivirus solution that uses machine learning to prevent malware and threats.

- **URL**: CylancePROTECT

4. **Symantec Endpoint Security**

- **Description**: Symantec Endpoint Security employs AI and machine learning for threat prevention, detection, and response.

- **URL**: Symantec Endpoint Security

5. **Trend Micro Apex One**

- **Description**: Trend Micro's Apex One uses AI to protect against advanced threats, offering endpoint security and detection capabilities.

- **URL**: Trend Micro Apex One

6. **McAfee MVISION**

- **Description**: McAfee MVISION employs AI and cloud-based threat detection to protect against cyber threats across endpoints, networks, and the cloud.

- **URL**: McAfee MVISION

7. **FireEye Helix**

    - **Description**: FireEye Helix offers AI-driven threat detection and response, along with security orchestration capabilities.
    - **URL**: FireEye Helix

8. **Vectra AI**

    - **Description**: Vectra AI provides network detection and response using AI to identify and respond to cyberattacks.
    - **URL**: Vectra AI

9. **Exabeam Security Management Platform**

    - **Description**: Exabeam's platform uses AI and machine learning for security information and event management (SIEM) and user and entity behavior analytics (UEBA).
    - **URL**: Exabeam Security Management Platform

10. **Fortinet FortiAI**

    - **Description**: Fortinet's FortiAI uses AI-driven threat detection and network security solutions.
    - **URL**: Fortinet FortiAI

These AI tools and platforms are at the forefront of cybersecurity and threat detection, helping organizations protect their digital assets and respond effectively to evolving cyber threats.

Automated Vulnerability Assessment

In the realm of cybersecurity, the importance of identifying and remediating vulnerabilities is crucial for the protection of digital assets and data. Automated Vulnerability Assessment, harnessing the power of Artificial Intelligence (AI) and machine learning, has become a vital component in contemporary cybersecurity practices. This approach is essential for adapting to the continuously evolving threat landscape, meeting stringent regulatory compliance, and establishing a proactive defense mechanism against potential breaches and security incidents.

AI significantly enhances the process of Automated Vulnerability Assessment. It automates the scanning and discovery of vulnerabilities in networks, systems, and applications. Machine learning models play a crucial role in assessing and prioritizing vulnerabilities based on risk, impact, and potential exploits. Furthermore, AI systems facilitate continuous monitoring, identifying new vulnerabilities as they emerge, thus maintaining a robust security posture.

The methods employed in Automated Vulnerability Assessment are varied and sophisticated. These include network scanning for open ports, misconfigurations, and known vulnerabilities; web application scanning to detect issues like SQL injection and cross-site scripting (XSS); static and dynamic code analysis for identifying software code vulnerabilities; and endpoint scanning where AI-powered agents monitor endpoints for security flaws.

The benefits of Automated Vulnerability Assessment are manifold. It enables the rapid and efficient assessment of large networks and complex applications. The precision of AI-driven assessments significantly reduces false positives, ensuring that remediation efforts are effectively focused on genuine vulnerabilities. This proactive identification and patching of vulnerabilities substantially minimize the window of opportunity for attackers.

However, challenges and considerations in Automated Vulnerability Assessment remain. While these tools are highly effective, they may not detect all vulnerabilities, potentially leading to false negatives. Managing and prioritizing a large volume of vulnerabilities can be daunting, often requiring human intervention. Additionally, organizations must strategically allocate resources for vulnerability remediation based on the assessment results.

Looking to the future, AI is set to play an even more pivotal role in enhancing the accuracy and intelligence of vulnerability assessments. The integration of Automated Vulnerability Assessment with broader cybersecurity automation workflows is anticipated. Furthermore, AI-driven systems are expected to advance in predicting potential vulnerabilities before they are exploited.

In conclusion, Automated Vulnerability Assessment is a foundational element of modern cybersecurity strategies, enabling organizations to stay resilient against evolving threats. As technology continues to advance and the threat landscape changes, the role of AI in vulnerability assessment is poised to grow, ensuring more robust defense mechanisms. This evolution of Automated Vulnerability Assessment promises more precise, efficient, and proactive cybersecurity measures in the future.

Here is a list of AI tools and platforms relevant to automated vulnerability assessment.

1. **Nessus**

   - **Description**: Nessus is a widely-used vulnerability assessment tool that offers automated scanning and reporting capabilities.

   - **URL**: Nessus

2. **Qualys**

   - **Description**: Qualys provides cloud-based vulnerability management and assessment tools powered by AI and machine learning.

   - **URL**: Qualys

3. **Nexpose by Rapid7**

- **Description**: Nexpose is an AI-powered vulnerability management tool that helps organizations discover and remediate vulnerabilities.
- **URL**: Nexpose

4. **OpenVAS**

   - **Description**: OpenVAS is an open-source vulnerability scanner that utilizes AI for automated network and application vulnerability assessments.
   - **URL**: OpenVAS

5. **Tenable.io**

   - **Description**: Tenable.io offers cloud-based vulnerability management and automated scanning solutions with AI-enhanced capabilities.
   - **URL**: Tenable.io

6. **Acunetix**

   - **Description**: Acunetix is a web application security tool that employs AI for automated scanning and vulnerability detection.
   - **URL**: Acunetix

7. **SecPod SanerNow**

   - **Description**: SanerNow provides AI-driven cybersecurity solutions, including vulnerability management and automated threat detection.
   - **URL**: SecPod SanerNow

8. **Netsparker**

   - **Description**: Netsparker is an AI-powered web application security scanner that automates the identification of vulnerabilities.
   - **URL**: Netsparker

9. **Rapid7 InsightVM**

   - **Description**: InsightVM is a vulnerability management solution that utilizes AI for automated risk assessment and remediation.
   - **URL**: Rapid7 InsightVM

10. **SentinelOne**

    - **Description**: SentinelOne offers AI-driven endpoint security that includes automated vulnerability assessment and remediation.
    - **URL**: SentinelOne

These AI tools and platforms play a crucial role in automating vulnerability assessment processes, helping organizations identify and address security weaknesses in their networks, systems, and applications efficiently. They are essential components of modern cybersecurity strategies.

AI in Compliance and Data Privacy

The ever-increasing volume of data and the growing complexity of regulatory requirements have made compliance and data privacy two of the most critical challenges for organizations across industries. Artificial Intelligence (AI) is emerging as a valuable tool for navigating this complex landscape. In this section, we'll explore how AI is transforming compliance management and data privacy practices.

1. **The Compliance and Data Privacy Challenge**

   - **Rising Regulations**: The digital age has brought forth a multitude of regulations, including GDPR, HIPAA, CCPA, and more, making compliance a complex endeavor.

   - **Data Explosion**: Organizations handle vast amounts of data, making it challenging to track, protect, and comply with data privacy regulations.

   - **Penalties and Reputational Risks**: Non-compliance can lead to hefty fines and damage an organization's reputation.

2. **AI-Driven Compliance Management**

   - **Automated Risk Assessment**: AI can analyze vast datasets to assess compliance risks and identify potential violations.

   - **Natural Language Processing (NLP)**: NLP algorithms help in understanding and extracting insights from complex legal documents and regulatory texts.

   - **Predictive Analytics**: AI models predict potential compliance issues and recommend proactive measures.

3. **Applications in Compliance and Data Privacy**

   - **Privacy Impact Assessments**: AI automates privacy impact assessments, helping organizations understand how data processing impacts privacy.

   - **Data Classification**: AI classifies data, ensuring sensitive information is appropriately handled and protected.

   - **Incident Response**: AI aids in real-time detection and response to data breaches and privacy incidents.

4. **Benefits of AI in Compliance and Data Privacy**

   - **Efficiency**: AI automates labor-intensive compliance tasks, reducing the time and effort required.

- **Accuracy**: AI-driven analysis is more precise and less prone to human error.

- **Scalability**: AI can handle large datasets and adapt to changing regulations effortlessly.

5. Challenges and Considerations

- **Interpretability**: Understanding the reasoning behind AI-driven compliance decisions can be challenging.

- **Data Privacy**: AI's use in compliance must also adhere to data privacy regulations, creating a delicate balance.

- **Human Oversight**: While AI can automate many compliance tasks, human experts are still needed for interpretation and decision-making.

6. Future Trends and Developments

- **AI for Automated Auditing**: AI will be used for automated auditing and continuous monitoring of compliance.

- **Privacy by Design**: AI will play a role in embedding privacy principles into the design of systems and processes.

- **Global Compliance Solutions**: AI will help organizations navigate the complexities of compliance in an increasingly globalized world.

7. Conclusion

- **AI-Powered Compliance**: AI is becoming a vital tool in managing compliance and data privacy, offering organizations efficient ways to stay compliant in a data-centric world.

- **Data Protection Imperative**: As data continues to be the lifeblood of organizations, leveraging AI for compliance and data privacy is no longer optional but a strategic necessity.

AI is redefining the way organizations approach compliance and data privacy. Its ability to automate tasks, analyze large datasets, and predict potential issues makes it an indispensable ally in the complex and ever-evolving world of regulatory compliance and data protection. As AI continues to mature, its role in these domains will only become more critical.

Ethical Implications of AI in Software Development

The integration of Artificial Intelligence (AI) into software development is transforming the field, but it also introduces a range of ethical challenges and considerations that require thorough examination. These challenges encompass issues of bias, transparency, accountability, privacy concerns, and the broader societal impact of AI.

One of the primary ethical concerns is algorithmic bias, where AI systems may inherit biases present in their training data, leading to unfair and discriminatory outcomes. This bias can disproportionately affect marginalized and vulnerable groups, raising significant concerns about fairness and equality. Another key issue is the lack of transparency and explainability in some AI models, often referred to as 'black-box' AI. This opacity can impede efforts to audit AI systems and hold them accountable for their decisions.

Privacy concerns are also paramount, as AI-driven applications frequently depend on extensive data collection, potentially compromising user privacy. Questions of informed consent arise, as users may not fully understand how their data is being used. The issue of accountability and responsibility in AI-driven software decisions further complicates the ethical landscape. It can be challenging to determine who is legally and ethically responsible for these decisions, and developers must take proactive steps to prevent AI systems from causing harm or making unethical choices.

AI's societal impact, such as potential job displacement and the exacerbation of the digital divide, is another area of ethical concern. These developments can further marginalize underserved communities, making it crucial to consider the broader societal implications of AI.

To address these challenges, ethical frameworks and principles such as fairness, transparency, accountability, and inclusivity are being developed. Industry organizations and governments are also working on guidelines for responsible AI development. Mitigation strategies include techniques to reduce bias, efforts to make AI models more interpretable, and robust data privacy measures.

Looking ahead, the need for regulatory frameworks and standards for AI in software development is becoming increasingly apparent. Comprehensive ethics education for developers and AI practitioners is essential to navigate these ethical challenges effectively. There is also a growing demand for tools and methodologies to assess the societal impact of AI systems.

In conclusion, while the integration of AI into software development offers tremendous potential, it also poses significant ethical challenges. Developers have a responsibility to ensure that their AI creations align with ethical principles and serve society's best interests. Navigating the ethical terrain of AI in software development is an ongoing journey, requiring collaboration among developers, policymakers, and society to strike a balance between innovation and ethics. This collaboration is crucial to ensure that AI-driven software acts as a force for good, minimizing harm and discrimination while contributing positively to our interconnected world.

Addressing Bias and Fairness in AI Applications

Bias in Artificial Intelligence (AI) applications is a pressing concern that has garnered significant attention in recent years. As AI systems increasingly influence our lives, it's imperative to recognize and mitigate biases that can lead to unfair and discriminatory outcomes. This section explores the importance of addressing bias and promoting fairness in AI applications.

1. Understanding Bias in AI

- **Data Bias**: Bias can enter AI systems through biased training data, leading to skewed decision-making.

- **Algorithmic Bias**: Some AI algorithms may inadvertently reinforce existing biases or stereotypes.

- **Fairness Definitions**: Defining fairness in AI is complex, as it involves making trade-offs between different notions of fairness.

2. The Impact of Bias

- **Discrimination**: Biased AI can result in discriminatory outcomes, affecting individuals and communities unfairly.

- **Reputation and Trust**: Bias in AI applications can erode trust in the technology and the organizations deploying it.

- **Legal and Ethical Concerns**: Biased AI can lead to legal and ethical challenges, potentially resulting in legal action and reputational damage.

3. Methods to Address Bias and Promote Fairness

- **Diverse and Representative Data**: Ensuring training data is diverse and representative of the population can reduce bias.

- **Bias Detection Tools**: AI developers can utilize bias detection tools to identify potential biases in their models.

- **Fairness-Aware Algorithms**: Algorithms that aim to balance fairness concerns can be employed in AI systems.

- **Regular Audits**: Regularly auditing AI systems for bias and fairness should be a standard practice.

- **Ethical Guidelines**: Adhering to ethical guidelines and principles for responsible AI development is crucial.

4. Ethical Considerations

- **Balancing Fairness**: Developers must strike a balance between fairness and other objectives, such as accuracy and efficiency.

- **Ethical Decision-Making**: Ethical considerations should be integrated into every stage of AI development, from data collection to deployment.

- **Human Oversight**: Human experts play a vital role in interpreting and addressing bias in AI systems.

5. Real-World Applications

- **Recruitment and Hiring**: AI in recruitment should be free from gender, racial, or other biases to ensure equal opportunities.

- **Criminal Justice**: Bias-free AI is critical in applications like risk assessment and sentencing recommendations.

- **Finance**: Financial AI should provide equitable access to credit and financial services.

- **Healthcare**: Medical AI should ensure unbiased diagnosis and treatment recommendations.

6. Challenges and Considerations

- **Trade-offs**: Achieving perfect fairness may require trade-offs with other goals, such as accuracy.

- **Bias Mitigation Costs**: Implementing bias mitigation measures can increase development costs and complexity.

- **Bias in Unstructured Data**: Addressing bias in unstructured data, such as text and images, poses unique challenges.

7. Future Trends and Developments

- **AI Fairness Research**: Ongoing research into AI fairness will yield improved algorithms and techniques.

- **Regulation**: Governments and regulatory bodies are considering AI ethics and fairness regulations.

- **Public Awareness**: Increasing public awareness of AI bias and fairness issues will drive change.

8. Conclusion

- **Responsibility of Developers**: Developers and organizations must take responsibility for addressing bias and promoting fairness in AI applications.

- **Ethical AI for a Better Future**: By addressing bias and striving for fairness, we can harness the potential of AI to create a more equitable and just society.

Addressing bias and promoting fairness in AI applications is not just a technological challenge but a moral imperative. It requires a concerted effort from developers, organizations, regulators, and society at large to ensure that AI technology benefits all and does not perpetuate harmful biases and discrimination.

The Future of Employment in the Age of AI-Driven Software Development

The advent of Artificial Intelligence (AI) has had a profound impact on various industries, including software development. As AI continues to advance, it inevitably reshapes the employment landscape within the field. This section explores the future of employment in the age of AI-driven software development, discussing both the challenges and opportunities it presents.

1. **Automation and Job Transformation**

   - **Routine Tasks**: AI is proficient at automating routine, repetitive tasks, such as code generation and testing.

   - **Job Transformation**: While some traditional software development tasks may be automated, new roles will emerge requiring AI expertise.

2. **AI-Augmented Software Development**

   - **Enhancing Productivity**: AI tools augment developers' capabilities, improving productivity and code quality.

   - **AI as a Collaborator**: Developers will work alongside AI systems, leveraging their insights and recommendations.

3. **Reskilling and Upskilling**

   - **Continuous Learning**: Software developers will need to engage in continuous learning to stay updated with AI technologies.

   - **AI Literacy**: Gaining AI literacy will become essential for software professionals.

4. **AI Ethics and Governance**

   - **AI Governance Roles**: AI-driven software development will necessitate roles focused on ethics, fairness, and compliance.

   - **Mitigating Bias**: Professionals will be needed to ensure AI systems are unbiased and adhere to ethical standards.

5. **Specialized AI Development Roles**

   - **AI Specialists**: Dedicated roles, such as AI engineers and AI model developers, will be in demand to create and maintain AI systems.

   - **AI Research**: Research into advanced AI algorithms and models will continue to grow as a field.

6. **Global Competition and Collaboration**

   - **Global Workforce**: Software development teams may become increasingly globalized, leveraging talent from around the world.

- **Collaboration Platforms**: Collaboration platforms and remote work tools will facilitate global teamwork.

7. The Role of Creativity and Problem-Solving

- **Human Ingenuity**: Creativity, problem-solving, and innovation will remain uniquely human strengths in software development.

- **Complex Projects**: AI may handle routine tasks, allowing human developers to focus on complex, creative projects.

8. Evolving Job Market

- **Demand for AI Skills**: Job opportunities will grow in AI-driven software development, but demand will vary across regions and industries.

- **Adaptability**: Professionals who can adapt to changing technology trends will thrive.

9. Societal Implications

- **Income Disparities**: Addressing potential income disparities resulting from automation will be a societal challenge.

- **Education and Access**: Ensuring equitable access to AI education and opportunities will be essential.

10. Conclusion

- **A Transformative Shift**: AI-driven software development is ushering in a transformative shift in employment within the field.

- **Opportunities and Challenges**: While automation poses challenges, it also opens up exciting opportunities for innovation and growth.

- **Human-Centric Development**: Human creativity, ethics, and problem-solving will continue to be at the heart of software development, ensuring that AI is a tool for augmentation, not replacement.

The future of employment in AI-driven software development is marked by a blend of automation and human ingenuity. Embracing AI technologies while fostering a culture of continuous learning and adaptability will be key to thriving in this evolving landscape. As AI becomes a ubiquitous presence in software development, it offers the potential for greater efficiency, innovation, and positive societal impact when harnessed responsibly and ethically.

Chapter 10: The Future of AI in Software Development

Emerging Trends and Technologies

The future of AI in software development is set to be both exciting and transformative, reshaping how software is conceived, created, and maintained. We are witnessing a shift towards AI-powered development tools, where Integrated Development Environments (IDEs) are enhanced with AI capabilities for code completion, bug detection, and real-time code suggestions. Alongside this, AI-driven tools are emerging to automatically refactor code, enhancing its readability, performance, and maintainability.

AI's role in code generation is expanding as well. Developers will soon be able to interact with AI models using natural language to generate code snippets or even entire programs. This advancement is complemented by the rise of low-code and no-code platforms, which are democratizing software development, allowing non-developers to create applications through intuitive, AI-driven interfaces.

In testing and quality assurance, AI is revolutionizing the field by automating test case generation and execution, thereby optimizing software quality. AI models are also being developed to predict potential bugs and vulnerabilities before software deployment, marking a significant step towards more proactive and efficient software development practices.

The integration of AI in DevOps and Continuous Integration/Continuous Deployment (CI/CD) processes is streamlining these operations. AI is being used to automate CI/CD pipelines, reduce errors, and facilitate continuous monitoring, providing real-time insights into software performance. This integration significantly enhances the efficiency and reliability of software deployment and maintenance.

Explainable AI (XAI) is addressing the challenges of AI's "black-box" nature by making AI models more interpretable and transparent. This is crucial not only for understanding AI-driven decisions but also for meeting regulatory compliance, especially in highly regulated industries.

AI's role in software security is growing, with AI being embedded in applications for real-time threat detection and mitigation. Additionally, AI-driven tools are continuously assessing software for vulnerabilities, enhancing the overall security of the digital infrastructure.

Personalization in software is being driven by AI algorithms, which tailor user experiences and content based on individual behavior and preferences. This is further augmented by advanced recommendation systems powered by AI, enhancing content discovery and user engagement.

Natural Language Processing (NLP) is another area where AI is making significant strides. AI-driven chatbots and virtual assistants are becoming integral to software applications, and AI is enabling software to understand and communicate in multiple languages effortlessly.

Edge AI is revolutionizing mobile and IoT devices by enabling on-device data processing. This not only improves responsiveness and privacy but also empowers wearable devices with advanced capabilities like health monitoring and gesture recognition.

The integration of quantum computing with AI is poised to unlock new potentials. Quantum machine learning will allow AI algorithms to solve complex problems much faster, and quantum encryption will enhance the security of AI systems and data.

As AI becomes more integrated into software development, ethical considerations and regulations are becoming increasingly important. Developers are starting to view AI systems as collaborative teammates, leveraging their strengths in data analysis and pattern recognition. This collaboration is unleashing AI's potential to revolutionize software development while keeping human creativity, ethics, and problem-solving at the core.

The future of AI in software development is brimming with opportunities for increased efficiency, innovation, and personalized user experiences. However, it is also accompanied by the responsibility of ethical development and risk mitigation. Embracing these trends and technologies will enable software developers to create a more intelligent, efficient, and user-centric software ecosystem.

The future of AI in software development holds the promise of increased efficiency, innovation, and personalized user experiences. However, it also comes with the responsibility of ensuring ethical development and mitigating potential risks. Embracing these emerging trends and technologies will empower software developers to create a more intelligent, efficient, and user-centric software ecosystem.

Potential Future Applications and Innovations

The evolution of Artificial Intelligence (AI) in software development continues to open doors to a multitude of potential applications and innovations. As AI technologies advance, their integration into software development processes will lead to transformative changes in various domains. In this section, we explore some of the exciting potential future applications and innovations in AI-driven software development.

1. **AI-Generated Synthetic Data**

- **Data Augmentation**: AI will create synthetic datasets to augment limited training data, facilitating the training of more robust and accurate machine learning models.

- **Privacy-Preserving Training**: AI-generated synthetic data can be used to train models while preserving the privacy of sensitive real-world data.

2. **AI-Enhanced User Experience**

- **Emotion Recognition**: AI-driven applications will recognize user emotions through facial and voice analysis, allowing for personalized and empathetic interactions.

- **Human-AI Collaboration**: AI will assist developers in creating software interfaces that adapt in real-time to user behavior and preferences.

3. AI-Driven Creativity

- **AI-Generated Art and Content**: AI algorithms will autonomously create artwork, music, and written content, pushing the boundaries of creative expression.

- **Innovative Design**: AI will assist designers in generating novel design concepts, layouts, and product prototypes.

4. AI in Debugging and Error Correction

- **Automated Bug Fixes**: AI will identify and automatically fix software bugs and issues, reducing the need for manual debugging.

- **Code Refactoring**: AI will intelligently refactor code to enhance its efficiency, readability, and maintainability.

5. AI-Powered Code Summarization

- **Code Documentation**: AI will automatically generate comprehensive and human-readable code summaries, aiding in understanding and maintaining complex software systems.

- **Knowledge Transfer**: AI will facilitate knowledge transfer among developers, making it easier for new team members to grasp existing codebases.

6. AI-Driven Continuous Improvement

- **Self-Adaptive Systems**: AI will enable software systems to adapt and optimize themselves based on real-time usage and performance data.

- **Predictive Maintenance**: AI will predict and prevent software failures, enhancing system reliability and availability.

7. AI-Enhanced Cybersecurity

- **Adaptive Threat Detection**: AI will continuously adapt to evolving cybersecurity threats, providing real-time threat detection and response.

- **Autonomous Security Measures**: AI-driven security systems will autonomously respond to and mitigate cyberattacks.

8. AI in Medicine and Healthcare Software

- **AI-Driven Drug Discovery**: AI will accelerate drug discovery processes, leading to the development of new treatments and medications.

- **Personalized Healthcare**: AI will enable the creation of highly personalized healthcare software, optimizing treatment plans for individual patients.

9. AI in Education Software

- **Personalized Learning**: AI will customize educational content and pathways for students, catering to their unique learning styles and abilities.

- **Automated Grading**: AI-driven systems will automate grading and assessment tasks, freeing educators to focus on teaching.

10. **AI for Space Exploration and Research**

- **Autonomous Rovers**: AI-driven software will enhance the autonomy of planetary rovers, enabling them to make independent decisions in real-time.

- **Data Analysis**: AI will analyze vast amounts of astronomical data, aiding in the discovery of new celestial phenomena.

- **AI Oversight**: Ethical AI governance models will oversee AI systems to ensure they adhere to ethical guidelines and regulatory standards.

- **AI Accountability**: AI systems will be held accountable for their decisions and actions, with mechanisms for recourse in case of harm.

- **Quantum Machine Learning**: The convergence of quantum computing and AI will lead to breakthroughs in solving complex problems and optimization tasks.

- **Quantum AI Security**: Quantum AI will bolster the security of AI systems through quantum-resistant encryption and authentication.

- **Limitless Possibilities**: The potential future applications and innovations of AI in software development are limitless, offering solutions to challenges we have yet to encounter.

- **Human-AI Synergy**: As AI becomes deeply integrated into software development, it will augment human creativity, enhance productivity, and lead to unprecedented innovations across industries.

The future of AI in software development holds remarkable promise, and as these potential applications and innovations continue to unfold, they will revolutionize the way we create, interact with, and benefit from software in our increasingly AI-augmented world.

Preparing for an AI-Augmented Software Development Landscape

The emergence of Artificial Intelligence (AI) as a pivotal force in software development brings with it both unprecedented opportunities and new challenges. To thrive in an AI-augmented software development landscape, individuals, organizations, and the industry as a whole must undertake a series of strategic preparations. In this section, we delve into the essential steps to prepare for a future where AI is an integral part of software development.

1. **Embrace Continuous Learning**

- **Stay Informed**: Keep abreast of the latest AI trends, technologies, and best practices through continuous learning and professional development.

- **AI Education**: Invest in AI education and training programs for yourself and your team to build AI literacy and expertise.

2. Cultivate Ethical AI Practices

- **Ethical Frameworks**: Develop and adhere to ethical guidelines that prioritize fairness, transparency, accountability, and bias mitigation in AI development.

- **Ethics Training**: Ensure that your development teams are well-versed in AI ethics and the responsible use of AI technologies.

3. Foster Collaborative Environments

- **Cross-Disciplinary Collaboration**: Encourage collaboration between software developers, data scientists, domain experts, and ethicists to harness the full potential of AI.

- **Team Diversity**: Build diverse teams with a range of perspectives and experiences to foster innovative AI solutions.

4. Adopt AI-Ready Infrastructure

- **Data Infrastructure**: Invest in robust data infrastructure to collect, store, and process data efficiently for AI applications.

- **Scalable Computing**: Ensure access to scalable computing resources, including cloud services and high-performance computing clusters.

5. AI Development Tools and Frameworks

- **Tool Selection**: Evaluate and select AI development tools and frameworks that align with your specific software development needs.

- **Open Source Community**: Leverage the vibrant AI open-source community for tools, libraries, and resources.

6. Test and Quality Assurance

- **AI Testing**: Develop testing strategies that encompass AI model validation, integration testing, and real-world scenario testing.

- **Quality Assurance**: Implement AI-powered quality assurance tools to ensure software reliability and performance.

7. AI-Driven DevOps

- **CI/CD Integration**: Integrate AI into your Continuous Integration and Continuous Deployment (CI/CD) pipelines to automate deployment and monitoring.

- **DevSecOps**: Incorporate AI-driven security and compliance checks into the DevOps process.

8. Adaptive Workforce Planning

- **Skill Development**: Plan for upskilling and reskilling your workforce to equip them with AI-related skills and knowledge.

- **Flexible Roles**: Be prepared to adapt job roles to incorporate AI responsibilities and new AI-centric positions.

9. Data Privacy and Security

- **Privacy by Design**: Prioritize data privacy and security by implementing privacy-preserving AI techniques and encryption protocols.

- **Regulatory Compliance**: Stay informed about evolving data protection regulations and ensure AI applications adhere to compliance requirements.

10. Innovation Culture

- **Risk-Taking**: Cultivate a culture that encourages experimentation and calculated risk-taking in AI development.

- **Failure Tolerance**: Acknowledge that not all AI projects will succeed, but they provide valuable learning opportunities.

- **Collaborative Ventures**: Collaborate with AI research institutions, startups, and industry partners to access cutting-edge AI technologies and expertise.

- **Ecosystem Participation**: Actively engage in AI-related industry associations and consortia to influence AI standards and practices.

- **Sharing Best Practices**: Contribute to the AI community by sharing your experiences, best practices, and insights through publications, forums, and conferences.

- **Mentoring**: Support the next generation of AI developers and practitioners through mentorship and knowledge sharing.

- **A Bright AI-Augmented Future**: The AI-augmented software development landscape promises innovation, efficiency, and transformative possibilities.

- **Proactive Preparation**: By proactively preparing for this future, individuals and organizations can harness the power of AI while ensuring ethical, secure, and inclusive software development practices.

The path to a successful AI-augmented software development landscape involves a commitment to lifelong learning, ethical principles, collaboration, and adaptability. By taking these steps, you can position yourself and your organization to thrive in a world where AI is an integral part of the software development process, and where innovation knows no bounds.

Conclusion

In the journey through the dynamic landscape of Artificial Intelligence (AI) in software development, we have explored the transformative power of AI, its applications across the software development lifecycle, and the profound impact it has on the future of this field. As we wrap up our exploration, let's recap the key insights and takeaways that have emerged and contemplate the ongoing evolution of AI in software development.

Recap of Key Insights and Takeaways

1. **AI Augmentation, Not Replacement**: AI is a powerful tool that augments human capabilities in software development rather than replacing them. It enhances productivity, automates repetitive tasks, and enables developers to focus on creativity and problem-solving.

2. **AI Across the Software Lifecycle**: AI's influence extends across the entire software development lifecycle, from requirements analysis and design to coding, testing, deployment, and maintenance.

3. **AI for Predictive Analytics**: Predictive analytics powered by AI helps project managers and teams make informed decisions, anticipate issues, and optimize resource allocation.

4. **AI in Team Collaboration and Communication**: AI tools enhance team collaboration and communication by automating routine tasks, providing data-driven insights, and facilitating real-time collaboration.

5. **AI in Continuous Integration/Continuous Deployment (CI/CD)**: AI streamlines CI/CD processes, improving efficiency, reducing errors, and enabling faster and more reliable software deployments.

6. **AI for Real-Time Monitoring and Maintenance**: AI ensures the reliability and performance of software through real-time monitoring, predictive maintenance, and automated issue resolution.

7. **AI in Cybersecurity and Threat Detection**: AI plays a crucial role in detecting and mitigating cybersecurity threats, providing a proactive defense against evolving cyberattacks.

8. **Automated Vulnerability Assessment**: AI-driven vulnerability assessment tools continuously scan and evaluate software for potential security weaknesses.

9. **AI in Compliance and Data Privacy**: AI helps organizations navigate complex regulatory landscapes by automating risk assessments, data classification, and privacy impact assessments.

10. **Ethical Considerations**: Ethical AI development is paramount, focusing on fairness, transparency, accountability, and bias mitigation throughout the software development process.

11. **Future of Employment**: AI transforms the employment landscape in software development, emphasizing the need for continuous learning, reskilling, and human-centric development.

12. **Emerging Trends and Technologies**: The future of AI in software development brings AI-powered development tools, code generation, quality assurance, AI ethics, and quantum computing, among others.

13. **Potential Future Applications and Innovations**: AI's potential is boundless, with applications in synthetic data generation, user experience enhancement, creativity, and more across various industries.

14. **Preparation for an AI-Augmented Landscape**: Preparing for AI in software development involves continuous learning, ethical AI practices, collaboration, infrastructure readiness, and fostering an innovation culture.

The Ongoing Evolution of AI in Software Development

The journey through AI in software development is far from over. AI continues to evolve, offering novel opportunities and challenges. As AI technologies become more sophisticated, we can anticipate:

- **More Advanced AI Tools**: AI tools will become even more advanced, simplifying complex tasks and providing deeper insights.

- **Enhanced AI Ethics and Governance**: Ethical AI practices and governance models will mature to ensure responsible AI development.

- **Greater Integration of AI**: AI will be seamlessly integrated into software development processes, becoming an indispensable part of every developer's toolkit.

- **Innovations Beyond Imagination**: The potential for AI-driven innovations across industries and applications is limitless.

In closing, the ongoing evolution of AI in software development represents a journey of transformation, empowerment, and innovation. As AI augments human creativity and problem-solving, it opens up new horizons for software development, paving the way for a future where software solutions are more intelligent, efficient, and user-centric. Embracing AI with ethics and diligence, we embark on this exciting voyage towards a brighter and more innovative future.

Appendices

Glossary of AI and Software Development Terms

In this glossary, you will find a compilation of key terms related to Artificial Intelligence (AI) and software development. Understanding these terms is essential for navigating the AI-augmented software development landscape.

1. **AI (Artificial Intelligence):** The simulation of human intelligence processes by machines, including learning, reasoning, problem-solving, and decision-making.

2. **Algorithm:** A set of rules or instructions for solving a specific problem or performing a particular task.

3. **Bias:** In AI, bias refers to systematic errors in algorithms or data that result in unfair or discriminatory outcomes.

4. **Chatbot:** A computer program designed to simulate human conversation, often used for customer support and information retrieval.

5. **Deep Learning:** A subfield of machine learning that focuses on artificial neural networks with multiple layers, enabling complex pattern recognition.

6. **DevOps:** A set of practices that combines software development (Dev) and IT operations (Ops) to automate and streamline software delivery and infrastructure management.

7. **Ethical AI:** The practice of developing AI systems that adhere to ethical principles, including fairness, transparency, accountability, and bias mitigation.

8. **Machine Learning (ML):** A subset of AI that involves the use of algorithms to enable computers to learn from and make predictions or decisions based on data.

9. **Natural Language Processing (NLP):** The field of AI that focuses on enabling computers to understand, interpret, and generate human language.

10. **Quantum Computing:** A type of computing that leverages the principles of quantum mechanics to perform complex calculations at exponentially faster speeds than classical computers.

11. **Reinforcement Learning:** A machine learning paradigm where an agent learns to make decisions by interacting with an environment and receiving rewards or punishments.

12. **Supervised Learning:** A machine learning approach where the model is trained on labeled data with known outcomes to make predictions on new, unseen data.

13. **Unsupervised Learning:** A machine learning approach where the model learns patterns and relationships in data without labeled outcomes.

14. **Version Control:** The practice of tracking changes to code and collaborating on software development using tools like Git.

Continuing your exploration of AI in software development and related topics is crucial for staying current and expanding your knowledge. Here are some recommended resources:

1. **Books**:

    - "Artificial Intelligence: A Guide to Intelligent Systems" by Michael Negnevitsky

    - "Deep Learning" by Ian Goodfellow, Yoshua Bengio, and Aaron Courville

    - "The DevOps Handbook" by Gene Kim, Patrick Debois, John Willis, and Jez Humble

2. **Online Courses and Tutorials**:

    - Coursera and edX offer courses on AI, machine learning, and software development.

    - YouTube channels like "3Blue1Brown" provide insightful tutorials on AI and mathematics behind it.

3. **AI Research Journals and Websites**:

    - Explore research papers and articles on AI from platforms like arXiv and Google AI.

    - Visit the official websites of organizations like OpenAI, Google AI, and Microsoft Research for the latest AI developments.

4. **AI Development Tools and Frameworks**:

    - Experiment with AI development using tools like TensorFlow, PyTorch, and scikit-learn.

    - Join AI communities on GitHub to collaborate and access open-source AI projects.

Interviews with Industry Experts

To gain deeper insights into the real-world applications of AI in software development and stay informed about industry trends, consider reading interviews with experts in the field. Here are a few notable experts you might want to follow:

1. **Andrew Ng**: Co-founder of Google Brain and Coursera, Andrew Ng is a prominent figure in AI education and research.

2. **Fei-Fei Li**: Professor at Stanford University and a leading expert in computer vision and AI ethics.

3. **Yann LeCun**: Chief AI Scientist at Facebook and a pioneer in deep learning and convolutional neural networks.

4. **Satya Nadella**: CEO of Microsoft, leading the company's initiatives in AI and cloud computing.

5. **Jeff Dean**: Senior Fellow at Google Research, known for his contributions to deep learning and large-scale distributed systems.

6. **Françoise Beaufays**: Principal Scientist at Google, specializing in natural language processing and speech recognition.

References

This section provides a comprehensive list of sources, references, and citations used during the research and composition of this book. These sources have contributed to the accuracy and depth of the content presented throughout the chapters.

1. Negnevitsky, M. (2005). "Artificial Intelligence: A Guide to Intelligent Systems." Pearson Education.

2. Goodfellow, I., Bengio, Y., & Courville, A. (2016). "Deep Learning." MIT Press.

3. Kim, G., Debois, P., Willis, J., & Humble, J. (2016). "The DevOps Handbook: How to Create World-Class Agility, Reliability, & Security in Technology Organizations." IT Revolution Press.

4. Coursera (https://www.coursera.org/): Online platform offering courses on AI, machine learning, and software development.

5. edX (https://www.edx.org/): Online platform providing courses on AI, machine learning, and software development.

6. 3Blue1Brown (https://www.youtube.com/c/3blue1brown): YouTube channel featuring tutorials on AI and mathematics.

7. arXiv (https://arxiv.org/): Online repository for research papers in AI and related fields.

8. OpenAI (https://www.openai.com/): Official website of OpenAI, an organization advancing AI research and development.

9. Google AI (https://ai.google/): Official website of Google AI, featuring research and projects in artificial intelligence.

10. Microsoft Research (https://www.microsoft.com/en-us/research/): Website showcasing research efforts in AI and computer science by Microsoft.

11. TensorFlow (https://www.tensorflow.org/): An open-source machine learning framework developed by Google.

12. PyTorch (https://pytorch.org/): An open-source deep learning framework maintained by Facebook's AI Research lab.

13. scikit-learn (https://scikit-learn.org/): An open-source machine learning library for Python.

14. GitHub (https://github.com/): Online platform for collaborative software development and access to open-source AI projects.